How to Develop Ir G000253592

Overcoming Common Problems Series

Selected titles

A full list of titles is available from Sheldon Press,
36 Causton Street, London SW1P 4ST and on our website at
www.sheldonpress.co.uk

Overcoming Common Problems Series

Coping with Heartburn and Reflux
Dr Tom Smith

Coping with Kidney Disease
Dr Tom Smith

Coping with Life after Stroke
Dr Mareeni Raymond

Coping with Life's Challenges: Moving on from adversity
Dr Windy Dryden

Coping with Phobias and Panic
Professor Kevin Gournay

Coping with PMS
Dr Farah Ahmed and Dr Emma Cordle

Coping with Polycystic Ovary Syndrome
Christine Craggs-Hinton

Coping with the Psychological Effects of Cancer
Professor Robert Bor, Dr Carina Eriksen and Ceilidh Stapelkamp

Coping with Radiotherapy
Dr Terry Priestman

Coping with Rheumatism and Arthritis
Dr Keith Souter

Coping with Snoring and Sleep Apnoea
Jill Eckersley

Coping with Suicide
Maggie Helen

Coping with Tinnitus
Christine Craggs-Hinton

Coping with Type 2 Diabetes
Susan Elliot-Wright

Coping with Your Partner's Death: Your bereavement guide
Geoff Billings

Depression: Healing emotional distress
Linda Hurcombe

Depressive Illness
Dr Tim Cantopher

Divorce and Separation: A legal guide for all couples
Dr Mary Welstead

Dynamic Breathing: How to manage your asthma
Dinah Bradley and Tania Clifton-Smith

Every Woman's Guide to Digestive Health
Jill Eckersley

The Fertility Handbook
Dr Philippa Kaye

The Fibromyalgia Healing Diet
Christine Craggs-Hinton

Free Yourself from Depression
Colin and Margaret Sutherland

A Guide to Anger Management
Mary Hartley

Helping Children Cope with Anxiety
Jill Eckersley

Helping Children Cope with Grief
Rosemary Wells

High-risk Body Size: Take control of your weight
Dr Funké Baffour

How to Beat Worry and Stress
Dr David Delvin

How to Cope with Difficult People
Alan Houel and Christian Godefroy

How to Develop Inner Strength
Dr Windy Dryden

How to Live with a Control Freak
Barbara Baker

How to Lower Your Blood Pressure: And keep it down
Christine Craggs-Hinton

How to Manage Chronic Fatigue
Christine Craggs-Hinton

Hysterectomy: Is it right for you?
Janet Wright

The IBS Healing Plan
Theresa Cheung

Living with Angina
Dr Tom Smith

Living with Asperger Syndrome
Dr Joan Gomez

Living with Autism
Fiona Marshall

Living with Bipolar Disorder
Dr Neel Burton

Living with Birthmarks and Blemishes
Gordon Lamont

Living with Crohn's Disease
Dr Joan Gomez

Living with Eczema
Jill Eckersley

Living with Fibromyalgia
Christine Craggs-Hinton

Living with Gluten Intolerance
Jane Feinmann

Living with Grief
Dr Tony Lake

Living with Loss and Grief
Julia Tugendhat

Living with Osteoarthritis
Dr Patricia Gilbert

Overcoming Common Problems Series

Overcoming Common Problems

How to Develop Inner Strength

DR WINDY DRYDEN

sheldon **PRESS**

First published in Great Britain in 2011

Sheldon Press
36 Causton Street
London SW1P 4ST
www.sheldonpress.co.uk

British Library Cataloguing-in-Publication Data

A catalogue record for this book is available from the British Library

ISBN 978–1–84709–133–8

1 3 5 7 9 10 8 6 4 2

Typeset by Fakenham Prepress Solutions, Fakenham, Norfolk NR21 8NN
Printed in Great Britain by Ashford Colour Press

Produced on paper from sustainable forests

Contents

1

The foundations of inner strength

Introduction

This book is about developing inner strength. By this I mean developing healthy responses to pressure from without and from within to take the easy way, but one which compromises your values and long-term goals. I am firmly of the view that no matter what your genetic heritage, upbringing or education, you can learn to develop inner strength. It would nice if doing so were easy, but sadly this is rarely the case. However, if this does not deter you and you are willing to put in the work by applying what you read in this book, then you should benefit from what I have to say.

Reading on its own won't help you. It's the same with gardening. If you have a garden and enjoy tending it you will know that reading about how to keep a garden looking nice will help you develop good ideas that you can apply to your garden. But reading a book is not sufficient for you to achieve this goal. You will know that a lot of hard work goes into keeping a garden fertile and looking nice. First, you need to prepare the ground and ensure that all weeds are uprooted. Second, you need to keep a watchful eye open for insects and animals that can potentially wreak havoc in your garden by infecting or eating your lovely plants and flowers. Third, you cannot rest on your laurels for too long because, if you do, your garden will not maintain itself. It will deteriorate through lack of ongoing care.

Inner strength is very much like a garden. It needs hard work to lay the solid foundations and regular care and attention to keep it blossoming. In this chapter, therefore, I will discuss the foundations of inner strength, and in the chapters that follow I will discuss how you can build on these foundations in various areas where inner strength is called for.

The foundations of inner strength are characterized by four attitudes or beliefs that need to be present if you are to deal with life's adversities in a healthy way. In this chapter, I will discuss these four attitudes or beliefs. However, let me first say a word about the approach on which this book is based.

This book is based on Rational-Emotive Cognitive Behavioural Therapy. You may have heard of Cognitive Behavioural Therapy (CBT), for it has entered into the public consciousness very much as psychoanalytic therapy did many years ago and you have probably heard CBT described as a therapeutic approach. However, in my view it is not a therapeutic approach but a therapeutic tradition in which there are a number of distinctive approaches, of which Rational Emotive Behavioural Therapy (known as REBT) is one. REBT was founded in 1955 by Dr Albert Ellis (1913–2007) and I will discuss the inner strength Dr Ellis drew on in order to get recognition for this approach. The term 'Rational-Emotive Cognitive Behavioural Therapy' (RECBT) – which I will use in this book to remind you of the book's roots – shows that the approach is placed within the CBT tradition and that its distinctive features are REBT in nature.

Flexible beliefs

In this section, I will discuss beliefs that are flexible in nature. However, I will first outline a number of basic facts about human beings.

- *We have desires for certain things to happen* We do not proceed in life free from desires, wants or wishes. Indeed, our desires are what make the world go around. Normally, when we consider something to be good or in our best interests we want it to happen.

- *We have desires for certain things not to happen* When we consider something to be bad or not in our best interests, then we don't want it to happen.
- *We have a broad range of desires* Unless we have tunnel vision our desires spread across a wide spectrum of events. Thus, we may want: (1) our local football team to win the league; (2) our children to be safe from harm; and (3) ourselves to be promoted at work.
- *Different people have different desires* Fortunately, we don't all want the same things. Indeed, the old adage 'different strokes for different folks' is particularly relevant in this area of human endeavour.
- *Our desires vary in strength* Some of our desires are strong, others are medium and yet others are weak. Thus, I may mildly want to beat you at a game of tiddlywinks, whereas I may very strongly want to be promoted at work.

Our desires can be kept flexible or made rigid

When you have a desire, say for success, then you can either keep this desire flexible or make it rigid. When you keep it flexible, you acknowledge that you want success, but you also realize that you do not have to achieve such success. You recognize that it is possible for you not to succeed and you incorporate this possibility into your belief system. Further, you recognize that there is a logical connection between wanting to succeed and believing that you don't have to do so. You also acknowledge that when you believe you want to succeed, but do not have to do so, then you will feel concerned but not anxious about the prospect of not succeeding, and will feel disappointed but not depressed if it turns out that you do not succeed. In other words, your negative emotions will be healthy rather than unhealthy, and these healthy negative emotions, as they are known in

RECBT, will help you (1) to process and learn from your failure to succeed and (2) to apply this learning to future achievement-related situations.

As I have also mentioned, it is possible for you to take your desires and make them rigid, and you are more likely to do this when your desires are strong than when they are moderate or mild. When you make your desires rigid, you take a desire (again for success) and you transform it into something that you think you must achieve. Thus you believe: 'I want to achieve success and therefore I have to do so.'

When you make your desire rigid, you are trying to exclude the possibility of not succeeding when that possibility in reality clearly exists. As such you are trying to make reality conform to your rigid belief rather than change your rigid belief to fit reality.

Further, you make an illogical connection between wanting to succeed and believing that you have to succeed. This is illogical: it really does not make sense for you to say that because you want something, therefore you have to have it.

Additionally, when you believe that because you want to succeed you have to do so, you will feel anxious rather than concerned about the prospect of not succeeding and depressed rather than disappointed if it turns out that you do not succeed. In other words, your negative emotions will be unhealthy rather than healthy and these unhealthy negative emotions, as they are known in RECBT, will get in the way of you processing and learning from your failure to succeed.

I hope you can see from this discussion that holding rigid beliefs will pose a significant obstacle to you developing inner strength in response to situations where you are tempted to take the easy way rather than the difficult path of pursuing your long-term goals. In contrast, holding flexible beliefs will help you to deal effectively with such temptations despite the fact that you will feel bad when doing so. It may surprise you that healthy

negative feelings such as concern, sadness, remorse, disappoint-
ment, sorrow and healthy anger, jealousy and envy constitute a
healthy feeling response to not giving in to these temptations.
They are a realistic feeling response when your desires are not
met and will also help give you the inner strength to stay on
the path towards reaching your long-term goals. This will be a
recurring theme in this book.

So your basic task here is to acknowledge your desires but to
convince yourself that you don't have to have these desires met,
no matter how important they are to you. If you truly believe
this, it will help you enormously to develop inner strength in
the face of urges to stray from the path towards your long-term
goals.

Non-awfulizing beliefs

When you hold a set of flexible beliefs which outline what you
want in life[1] but do not demand that you get and you encounter
some kind of obstacle to what you want, then you will make
some kind of negative evaluation of this situation. You will
think that it is bad or unfortunate that you are facing such an
obstacle. However, if your evaluation is non-extreme then you
will not think that it is terrible, awful or the end of the world
that the obstacle has occurred. Having said this, the negativity
of your evaluation will depend on the strength of your unmet
desire, as shown in the following statements:

> I very much wanted to get that promotion, but sadly I did not
> have to get it. It is very bad that I was not promoted, but it is not
> the end of the world.

> I moderately wanted to be picked for the first team, but it
> wasn't necessary that I was. It is bad not to be selected, but
> not terrible.

---

[1] Throughout this book when I talk about 'what you want in life', I mean (1) the
presence of desired conditions and (2) the absence of negative conditions.

I mildly wanted to beat you at tiddlywinks, but it was not essential that I did. It is slightly bad that you beat me, but hardly awful.

Your negative evaluations can be extreme or non-extreme

As I have shown above, when you hold flexible beliefs then your negative evaluations of situations where you don't get what you want (but do not need) are non-extreme. Even when your desire is very strong, when you hold them flexibly then your evaluations may be very negative, but they are still not extreme. They are not extreme because you are stating that they are *not* awful, terrible, or the end of the world.

However, you can make these negative evaluations extreme by transforming your flexible beliefs into rigid beliefs. As shown above, you particularly tend to do this when your desires are strong, as shown below:

Since I very much wanted to get that promotion, I absolutely should have got it and it is the end of the world that I didn't.

Non-extreme negative evaluations are known as non-awfulizing beliefs. They are rational for three reasons:

1 *Non-awfulizing beliefs are true* Non-awfulizing beliefs are true because you acknowledge that no matter how bad it is to be deprived of what you want, it could be worse and therefore it is not terrible. As Smokey Robinson's mother used to tell her son: 'From the day you are born till you ride in the hearse, there's nothing so bad that it couldn't be worse.'
2 *Non-awfulizing beliefs are sensible* You recognize that there is a logical connection between it being bad not to get what you want and it not being awful.
3 *Non-awfulizing beliefs are constructive* When you believe that it is bad not to succeed, for example, but that it is not awful if this happens, then you will once again feel concerned but not anxious about the prospect of not succeeding,

and disappointed but not depressed if it turns out that you do not succeed. In other words, your negative emotions will be healthy rather than unhealthy and these healthy negative emotions, as they are known in RECBT, will help you (1) to process and learn from your failure to succeed and (2) to apply this learning to future success-related situations.

Transforming negative evaluations into awfulizing beliefs

When your non-extreme evaluations are particularly negative it is easy for you to transform them into extreme awfulizing beliefs. Thus you believe: 'It is very bad if I do not succeed and therefore it would be awful if this were to happen.'

When you make a negative evaluation extreme, your resultant awfulizing belief implies that nothing could be worse than not having your needs met.

Further, you make an illogical connection between it being bad not getting what you want (and think that you need) and it thus being awful. If you think about it, it really does not follow that because it is bad to be deprived of what you want (but do not need), it is therefore awful for this to happen.

Additionally, when you believe it is terrible not to succeed, you will feel anxious rather than concerned about the prospect of not succeeding and depressed rather than disappointed if it turns out that you do not succeed. In other words, your negative emotions will be unhealthy rather than healthy, and these unhealthy negative emotions will get in the way of you processing and learning from your failure to succeed.

Again, I hope you can see from this discussion that holding awfulizing beliefs will pose a significant obstacle to you dealing effectively with threats to you staying on the path towards your long-term goals. By contrast, holding non-awfulizing beliefs will help you to deal effectively with these threats despite the fact that you will feel bad when you go against your short-term goals.

So your basic task here is to acknowledge that it is bad when your desires are not met, but that it is not the end of the world when this happens, no matter how important your desires are to you. If you truly believe this, this will again help you to develop inner strength in the face of adversity.

Discomfort tolerance beliefs

When you hold a set of flexible beliefs which outline what you want in life, but do not demand that you get, and you encounter some kind of obstacle to what you want, then your appraisal of your ability to tolerate the ensuing discomfort will be realistic. You will tend to think that while it will be a struggle for you to tolerate this discomfort, you will be able to tolerate it and it is worth it to you to do so. The degree of struggle you will experience in tolerating the discomfort when you don't get what you want, but don't need, will again depend on the strength of your unmet desire. Basically, the stronger your unmet desire under these conditions, the more you will struggle to tolerate the discomfort. However, assuming that your belief about getting what you want is flexible and you don't make it rigid by demanding that you must get what you want, then no matter how much you struggle to cope with the discomfort of not getting what you want you will be able to tolerate this discomfort and will believe that you will be able to do so, as shown below:

> I very much wanted to get that promotion, but sadly I did not have to get it. It is very difficult for me to tolerate not getting promoted, but I can tolerate it and it is worth it to me to do so.

Discomfort tolerance beliefs vs discomfort intolerance beliefs

As I have shown above, when you hold flexible beliefs then you will be able to tolerate the discomfort of not getting what you want even though it will be a struggle for you to do so. This holds no matter how strong your unmet desire is. Thus, your discomfort tolerance belief is non-extreme because you acknowledge struggle and you are able to tolerate discomfort.

However, when you transform your flexible beliefs into rigid beliefs, you also transform your non-extreme discomfort tolerance beliefs into extreme discomfort intolerance beliefs. You particularly tend to do this when your desires are strong, as shown below:

> Since I very much wanted to get that promotion, I absolutely should have got it and I can't bear it that I didn't.

But first let me consider why discomfort tolerance beliefs are regarded to be rational in RECBT. They are rational for three reasons:

1 *Discomfort tolerant beliefs are true* Discomfort tolerance beliefs are true because you acknowledge that no matter how much of a struggle it is for you to tolerate the discomfort when you are deprived of what you want, you can tolerate it and it is worth it to you to do so.

2 *Discomfort tolerance beliefs are sensible* You recognize that there is a logical connection between it being a struggle to tolerate the discomfort of not getting what you want and being able to tolerate it.

3 *Discomfort tolerance beliefs are constructive* When you believe that it is a struggle tolerating not succeeding, for example, but that you can tolerate it, you will again feel concerned but not anxious about the prospect of not succeeding, and disappointed but not depressed if it turns out that you do not succeed. As is the case with flexible beliefs and

non-awfulizing beliefs, holding discomfort tolerance beliefs about your unmet desires will lead you to feel negative emotions that will be healthy rather than unhealthy and, as I have pointed out before, these will help you to process and learn from your failure to succeed and to apply this learning to future success-related situations.

When you transform your discomfort tolerance belief into a discomfort intolerance belief, which particularly happens when your unmet desire is strong, then you think that you will die or disintegrate, which is obviously false.

Further, when you hold a discomfort intolerance belief you make an illogical connection between it being a struggle to tolerate not getting what you want (and think that you need) and it being intolerable. If you think about it, it really does not follow that because it is a struggle to tolerate being deprived of what you want (but do not need), it would therefore be intolerable were this to happen.

Additionally, when you believe that it is intolerable not to succeed you will feel anxious rather than concerned about the prospect of not succeeding, and depressed rather than disappointed if it turns out that you do not succeed. These unhealthy negative emotions will, as we have seen, get in the way of you processing and learning from your failure to succeed.

Again, I hope you can see from this discussion that holding discomfort intolerance beliefs will pose a significant obstacle to you dealing effectively with threats to working to achieve your long-term goals. By contrast, holding discomfort tolerance beliefs will help you to deal effectively with these threats despite the fact that you will feel badly when you don't act according to your short-term goals.

So your basic task here is to acknowledge that it is a struggle for you to put up with the discomfort of not having your desires met but that you can put up with it, no matter how important your desires are to you, and it is worth it to you to do so. Again, if you truly believe this, it will very much help you to develop inner strength in the face of challenges to you keeling along the path towards your long-term goals.

Acceptance beliefs

When you hold a set of flexible beliefs which outline what you want in life, but do not demand that you get, and you encounter some kind of obstacle to what you want, then you will accept yourself, others or life in general depending on who or what you consider responsible for the obstacle. You will tend to evaluate negatively your own behaviour if you think that you are responsible for the obstacle, but you will accept yourself as a complex, unrateable, fallible human being. This is also the case if you hold another person responsible, or life in general. You will negatively rate the relevant aspect of the other person or of life in general that is the source of you not getting what you want, but will refrain from giving the person or life a global negative rating. Rather, you will accept the other person as a complex, unrateable, fallible human being and you will accept life as being a highly complex mixture of the good, the bad and the neutral, too complex to merit a global rating.

While it is harder to develop and maintain acceptance beliefs when your unmet desires are strong, it is possible to do so, as shown below with reference to a self-acceptance belief.

> I very much wanted to get that promotion, but sadly I did not have to get it. While I am responsible for not getting it because my application was poor, I am not a bad person. I am a complex, unrateable, fallible human being who behaved poorly on this occasion.

Acceptance beliefs vs depreciation beliefs

As I have shown above, when you hold flexible beliefs then you will be able to accept yourself, others or life when you don't get what you want, no matter who or what was responsible for this.

This is the case no matter how strong your unmet desire. Thus, your acceptance belief is non-extreme because you rate what someone else did (for example) that was responsible for you not getting promoted, but you refrain from rating the whole of that person negatively.

However, when you transform your flexible beliefs into rigid beliefs, you also transform your non-extreme acceptance beliefs into extreme depreciation beliefs. You particularly tend to do this when your desires are strong, as shown below:

> Since I very much wanted to get that promotion, I absolutely should have got it and I am worthless for putting in a poor application.

But first let me consider why acceptance beliefs are regarded to be rational in RECBT. They are rational for three reasons:

1 *Acceptance beliefs are true* Acceptance beliefs are true because you acknowledge that no matter how badly you behave, your behaviour realistically does not define you as a person.[2] You can prove as a human being that you are:

● unique;
● too complex to warrant a global rating;
● fallible;
● in flux.

These four aspects are central elements of a self-acceptance belief.

2 *Acceptance beliefs are sensible* You recognize that there is a logical connection between one of your aspects being bad and you being a fallible, unique, unrateable human being constantly in flux. You acknowledge that the whole of you incorporates the part rather being defined by it.

---

[2] In this chapter, the points that I make about self-acceptance beliefs also apply to other-acceptance beliefs and life-acceptance beliefs.

3 *Acceptance beliefs are constructive* When you believe that you are an unrateable, fallible human being for not succeeding, for example, then yet again you will feel concerned but not anxious about the prospect of not succeeding, and disappointed but not depressed if it turns out that you do not succeed. As is the case with flexible beliefs, non-awfulizing beliefs and discomfort tolerance beliefs, holding acceptance beliefs about your unmet desires will lead you to feel negative emotions that will be healthy rather than unhealthy, and as I have pointed out several times before in this chapter, these emotions will help you to process and learn from you not getting what you want, and to apply this learning to future success-related situations.

When you transform your acceptance belief into a depreciation belief, which particularly happens when your unmet desire is strong, then you think that you are bad, worthless or less worthy as a person. This implies that your worth as a person can be defined by your behaviour, which is obviously false.

Further, when you hold a depreciation belief you make an illogical connection between your behaviour and you as a person. This is called the part–whole error in logic, where you incorrectly and nonsensically define the whole on the basis of a part.

Additionally, when you believe that you are worthless when you don't succeed, you will feel anxious rather than concerned about the prospect of not succeeding, and depressed rather than disappointed if it turns out that you do not succeed. These unhealthy negative emotions will, as we have seen several times already in this chapter, get in the way of you processing and learning from you not getting what you want.

Again, I hope you can see from this discussion that holding depreciation beliefs will pose a significant obstacle to you dealing effectively with threats to staying on the path towards your long-term goals. By contrast, holding acceptance beliefs will help you to deal effectively with these threats despite the fact that you will feel bad when you don't get what you want in the short term.

Thus, your basic task here is to convince yourself that:

- when you do not get your desires met and you are responsible for this, then this is bad, but you can still accept yourself as an unrateable, fallible human being;
- when you do not get your desires met and someone else is responsible for this, then this is bad, but you can still accept that person as an unrateable, fallible human being;
- when you do not get your desires met and life conditions are responsible for this, then this is bad, but you can still accept life as a complex mixture of good, bad and neutral events.

You can do this, no matter how important your thwarted desires are to you. Once again, if you truly believe this, it will help you enormously to develop inner strength in the face of threats to staying on the path towards your long-term goals.

Summary

If you are going develop inner strength, it is important that you lay down and maintain a set of beliefs that will enable you to do this in all areas of life where your goals are blocked and your short-term desires are not met. These beliefs are known in RECBT as: flexible beliefs, non-awfulizing beliefs, discomfort tolerance beliefs and acceptance beliefs. Thus, when your important desires are not met, for example, you will react in a healthy way when:

- you prefer, but do not demand, that this must not happen;
- you acknowledge the badness of this state of affairs, but take the horror out of it;
- you struggle to withstand not getting what you want, but recognize that you can withstand it and that it is worth it to you to do so;

- you accept yourself, others and/or life for frustrating your desires.

When you hold these beliefs in the face of urges to satisfy your short-term desires and thus not achieve your long-term goals, you will still experience negative emotions when you forgo the experience of short-term pleasure or where you decide to experience short-term discomfort as you choose to pursue your longer-term goals. However, these feelings will encourage you to implement the attitude of inner strength and will help you to deal with these challenges effectively.

Please keep these four healthy beliefs in mind as I discuss inner strength in a variety of domains beginning with self-motivation, which is the focus of the following chapter.

2

How to motivate yourself

Introduction

'I couldn't be bothered to do it. I just didn't have the motivation.'

How many times have you heard people say this? You may even have said it yourself. Motivation, it seems, is an important thing to have in your life.

In this chapter, I will be looking at self-motivation, and how it can be developed and maintained. But first, let's see what happens when instead of being self-motivated, the motivation comes from outside yourself – from other people.

The problem of being motivated by others

When someone else motivates you to do something, it may well be an effective inducement for you to do it. It could be someone you respect or admire, someone who inspires you. This kind of motivation may just be what you need to get you going, and having got started you may well have no problem in continuing to be motivated over a long period of time. In that case, keep doing what you're doing. The problem is, this is frequently not what happens.

What generally happens is that if it's not you doing the motivating and someone else is doing it for you, you will come to depend upon that person to get you going and then assume that, for you to act, he or she has to motivate you, even where taking such action is the best thing for you. In situations like these, if your motivator doesn't happen to be present or gets tired of motivating you and is not prepared to keep doing it, you are likely either to give up altogether or to search for another motivator. Instead of doing either of these, wouldn't it make much more sense for you to motivate yourself?

Janice did very well when she was at secondary school, but only because her mother Iris regularly insisted that she did her homework. When Janice came home from school Iris wouldn't let her do anything else until she had completed it. Having started, Janice usually got stuck into it, but never acquired the ability to motivate herself to do her homework. Invariably she depended on the motivation coming from her mother.

It was only when Janice went to university that her lack of self-motivation was critically exposed – not at the social level, as she quickly made friends, but academically. She began falling behind with her essays as she was unable to drive herself to get the required work done. Although she kept meaning and hoping to get on with her work, she had left it much too late and finally failed all her exams.

Janice's reliance on her mother to motivate her illustrates just how important self-motivation can be. So what do you need to do to motivate yourself? In this chapter we will be considering the key factors, including:

1 self-motivation and reasons
2 self-motivation and feelings
3 self-motivation and the hierarchy of needs.

Self-motivation and reasons

Probably the most powerful way to motivate yourself, in my opinion, is by having a good reason for doing so. If you think about it, you will see that such a reason is a thought or a way of thinking, but like so many thoughts it can be associated with a feeling and a tendency to act in a particular way. For example, the reason Sandra took on a second job was because the additional money would help her pay towards what she called her 'dream holiday' to Brazil. Whenever she reminded herself about this reason, it made her feel positive about the money (if not the work she had to do to earn it) and motivated her to get up and go to work on her one day off, when it would have been so much easier for her not to. Note the phrase 'when she reminded herself about this reason' as this is a vital point. While it is important to have good reasons for doing something, if you don't remind yourself about this reason then it may not be effective in helping to motivate yourself.

Thus, reminding yourself about the reasons for doing something will help nurture in you the inner strength you need to resist the temptation to do something that in the short term may seem to be more enjoyable.

Goals and reasons

As we have seen, the reason Sandra had taken on extra work was to save up for a holiday in Brazil. Her goal, therefore, was to earn extra money, while the reason for pursuing this goal was her holiday. If Sandra had taken on additional work purely to earn more money but there was no reason for her doing so, then she would certainly have found it more difficult to motivate herself to undertake the additional work than if she had a good reason to do so. As this demonstrates, reasons and goals are closely linked, and it will be of immense help to you if you bear both of these in mind as they constitute a basic step in increasing your chances of becoming self-motivated over a period of time.

It is important to note that there are two kinds of goals: positive and negative. Positive goals represent the presence of something you want, while negative goals represent the absence of something you don't want.

Negative and positive goals

With goals that are positive, our motivation to attain them will tend to be stronger than for those that are negative, given that all else is equal. This is because, with positive goals, it is easier to work towards something when you can clearly see what you are aiming for than it is with negative goals when you can't. Therefore, state what it is that you wish to achieve and then be honest with yourself about your reasons for working to achieve it.

Whose goals?

You need to distinguish between your own goals ('freely chosen goals'), goals that for some reason have been imposed on you ('imposed goals') and those you regard as your own but which you may have taken from other people without questioning them ('introjected goals'). Clearly, your chances of motivating yourself will be greatest when you freely choose your own goals, and you are least likely to motivate yourself when other people have imposed these goals on you. In my experience the clients who are least likely to work at the process of personal development and change, and therefore benefit least from it, are those who have been instructed to visit me to work on a problem which has been defined not by the client him or herself but by the other person. In such cases the client may not even necessarily accept or agree that he or she has the problem that has been thus defined. However, in order to appease the other person, the client will visit me, generally for a short period of time and then go away again, having fulfilled an obligation – not to him or herself but to the other person.

People who have introjected goals may initially be successful in pursuing them, but when things start to get difficult their self-motivation is inclined to disappear. This is because their goals were never really their own, and therefore when they come up against obstacles their self-motivation is too weak to overcome these hurdles.

To determine whether your goals are chosen freely or introjected, I suggest you do as follows. Write a list of your goals on a sheet of paper. Now write a list of the people who want you to achieve these goals and ask yourself this question:

Would I carry on pursuing the goals I have specified if these people were not bothered whether or not I achieved them or were even against my achieving them?

If you answer 'yes', you can be confident that these goals are your own and that they are ones you have freely chosen, but if you answer 'no' your goals are likely to be introjected.

> Alan's school careers advisor asked him what his career goals were. He responded that he wanted to become a baker like his father. On leaving school, he joined the family business, working in the bakery, but it wasn't long before he realized that his heart wasn't in it. Then, suddenly his father died and his mother told him that he should only take charge of the bakery if it was something he really wanted to do – that he should do whatever was right for him. Alan realized that what he had always wanted was to study medicine at university, and that while he thought he had wanted to join the bakery in reality he had only done so because it was what his father wanted of him.

Goals: process vs outcome

Up to this point we have been considering outcome goals: that is, the outcome of goal-directed behaviour. For instance, in the above situation Alan's outcome goal was to become a doctor. We have seen how self-motivation to achieve outcome goals is strongest when these goals are arrived at freely by the person him or herself and are what he or she (in this case, Alan) truly wants to achieve. Moreover, in the context of self-motivation, we need to bear in mind the person's relationship with whatever it is he or she needs to do to achieve these outcome goals. I call this the process of goal achievement.

When a process is not enjoyable If someone is highly committed to his or her outcome goals and enjoys the actual process of working towards them, that person is likely to have strong self-motivation. If Alan, for instance, is really serious about becoming a doctor and also enjoys studying, he will look forward to engaging in the process of becoming a doctor.

Even if the person doesn't enjoy this process, with strong commitment to those outcome goals he or she will be more likely to self-motivate in engaging in this process than if his or her commitment to such goals is only moderate or weak.

Jack, one of Alan's fellow students, also wanted to become a doctor, and was even hoping to make it as a surgeon. However, unlike Alan, he found the theoretical parts of the course boring and he wasn't keen on having to do all the academic work that was essential to studying medicine. While Jack worked just as hard as Alan on his studies, he had to force himself to do so; Alan, in comparison, actually enjoyed and looked forward to doing the academic parts of the course.

From this, you can see that if you have a strong commitment to your outcome goal but don't enjoy the actual process of working towards it, then to keep motivating yourself you have to remember, and continually remind yourself, why you are engaged in the process. If you concentrate on the reasons your goals are important for you to achieve, they will carry you through a process that you may not necessarily enjoy. This applies in particular to situations about which you may hold a discomfort tolerance belief. As we saw in the previous chapter, a discomfort tolerance belief is one in which, although you would have preferred to enjoy the process of working towards your goals, it is not necessary for you to do so and you are able to tolerate not enjoying the process of working towards your goals, particularly if it is worth your while to do so.

Goals, reasons and time-frames

You may have a large number of different goals throughout your life, some of them long-term, others short-term. People tend to prefer the latter, as short-term goals are often more pleasurable, and we may choose to pursue these rather than longer-term goals, especially when long-term goals are more difficult to achieve. However, if you decide to make your long-term goals your priority, you may also achieve some of your short-term goals at the same time if you plan carefully. To do so you will need to adopt a discomfort tolerance belief such as: 'I would like to have my short-term goals met, but I don't have to do so. I can pursue some of my short-term goals as long as doing so doesn't interfere with the pursuit of my long-term goals which are important to me.' Having a belief such as this will strengthen your motivation to fulfil both your long-term and short-term goals.

One reason or several

Up until now in this chapter the assumption has been that you have only one reason to pursue a goal. However, you may have several reasons and the more you can remind yourself about all these reasons, the greater will be your motivation to pursue your goals, especially if they are positive reasons, based firmly on your values, which is something we will be considering later in this chapter.

If you do have several reasons for pursuing a goal, these reasons may be quite varied. For example, Keith has a spare-time job as a stage hand in a youth theatre. Although genuinely interested not only in the theatre but also in working with young people, he also reckons it will be an excellent way to meet women, as a majority of the theatre staff are female. Frequently we may have a mixture of selfish and altruistic reasons for pursuing a goal. After all, few of us are saints and none of us is perfect! As long as you appreciate this and don't have unreasonable expectations of yourself that you can only do things for selfless reasons, you will be able to summon the motivation to pursue your goal.

Reasons: motivational power based on principles and values

When motivation is based upon values or principles that are important to you, this can be one of the strongest possible forms of self-motivation. Although some people regard the terms 'values' and 'principles' as being synonymous, they don't mean the same thing.

A *value* is an established ideal of life, while a *principle* is a fundamental belief, rule of action or conduct, a truth that is a foundation for other truths. A principle, in this context, may be said to be more basic than a value and even to underpin it. However, the important thing is for you to use these terms in ways that have meaning for you. Essentially, if you want to motivate yourself to do something, the best approach is to find a value or principle that underlies your selected course of action. For example, I am often asked what motivates me to write or edit so many books.[3] Apart from enjoying the writing process, what I'm really motivated by is my principle of helping people live healthy, happy lives. Sometimes, when I don't feel like writing, one of the ways for me to get back on track is to remind myself of this principle.

Thus, an effective way to develop inner strength when it comes to self-motivation is to keep reminding yourself of the values and principles that are the foundation of your long-term goals.

The reasons for not always acting on principles or values

Sometimes you may not act in accordance with your values or principles. For instance:

1 You may not consider your underlying value or principle during the course of your actions. If so, it is useful to remind yourself of this value or principle.

2 Your motivation may be to fulfil a short-term goal which is not in accordance with your value or principle. If so, remind yourself that it isn't necessary for you to achieve your short-term goal instantly, but that you can wait until you have acted in accordance with your value or principle.

---

[3] A total of 180 at the last count.

3 Your judgement regarding satisfying desire-based short-term goals or undertaking value-based actions to achieve longer-term goals may be affected by your use of drugs or alcohol. Such substances will increase the chances that you will wish to satisfy short-term goals, since they have a disinhibiting effect and fuel discomfort intolerance beliefs. If you wish to motivate yourself to engage in value-based activity, you should forgo the use of drugs and alcohol.

Self-motivation and feelings

Apart from using principles and values to motivate yourself, the other powerful way is through your feeling states. It is popularly considered that motivation is defined by the idea that we wish to do something. We describe this wish in saying we 'feel like' doing something. So when you haven't done something which it is in your interests to do, you claim that you did not do it because you did not 'feel like' doing it. This suggests that 'feeling like' doing something is motivation enough for acting in a certain way. My opinion, however, is that it isn't and that there are drawbacks to 'feeling-based' motivation.

On the other hand, 'feeling-based' motivation is not problematic in itself, particularly if you have a flexible view about such motivation. If you 'feel like' doing something and there's good reason to do it, your 'feeling-based' and 'reason-based' motivation can work together and form a powerful motivational combination. But when these different types of motivation conflict, the healthy approach is to accept that there's a conflict and decide which type you should allow yourself to be guided by at that particular time, according to which of them is in your best interests. This will tend to be the longer-term 'reason-based' motivation, particularly when your reasons are based on values or principles that are both well-founded and cherished.

If you decide to be guided by feeling-based motivation, you are unlikely to develop inner strength because the development of this quality often depends on acting against your instant feelings in favour of the long-term good.

Self-motivation and Maslow's hierarchy of needs

Among the best-known psychological theories is Abraham Maslow's theory of self-actualization (1968) which holds that humans naturally tend to 'actualize' themselves (i.e. develop their potential if certain conditions exist). He argued that humans have a variety of needs, which can be viewed as being organized hierarchically. People tend to be motivated to meet their lower-order needs first, before they strive to meet their higher-order needs.

In the pyramid diagram illustrating Maslow's hierarchy of needs (see Figure 2.1), our most primitive needs are physiological: breathing, food, water, sex, sleep, homeostasis and excretion. The next level up consists of our safety-based needs: physical security and security of employment, resources, family, health and property. The intermediate level is related to our needs for love and belonging – particularly friendship, family and sexual intimacy. Next there are our needs for esteem – self-esteem, confidence, achievement, respect of others and respect by others. Finally, at the apex of the pyramid are our self-actualization needs, which consist of morality, creativity, spontaneity, problem-solving, lack of prejudice and acceptance of facts.

Maslow generally argues that you are motivated to meet lower-level needs which are biologically based – for example, the need for food and shelter – before you will be motivated to meet higher esteem-based or self-actualization-based needs.

This is not always true, however. For example, I recently went to Yad Vashem in Jerusalem (the world's premier site for the commemoration of the Holocaust) and saw an example of

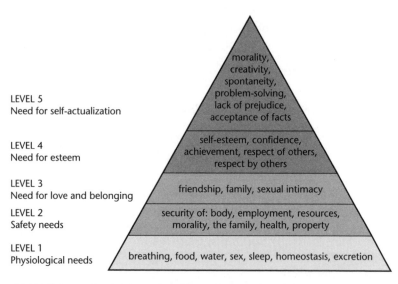

LEVEL 5
Need for self-actualization

LEVEL 4
Need for esteem

LEVEL 3
Need for love and belonging

LEVEL 2
Safety needs

LEVEL 1
Physiological needs

morality,
creativity,
spontaneity,
problem-solving,
lack of prejudice,
acceptance of facts

self-esteem, confidence,
achievement, respect of others,
respect by others

friendship, family, sexual intimacy

security of: body, employment, resources,
morality, the family, health, property

breathing, food, water, sex, sleep, homeostasis, excretion

Figure 2.1 Maslow's hierarchy of needs, represented as a pyramid with the more basic needs at the bottom.

beautiful embroidery done by women in a concentration camp. This prompts the question: what would motivate people to be creative when they had been robbed of their freedom and were starving? The answer must be the desire of the human spirit not to be crushed even in the most horrendous circumstances, and it demonstrates how people can develop and show great inner strength in the most appalling environments. If you bear this in mind, and remember the beautiful embroidery of these women, it may inspire you to summon up the inner strength when you need to do so.

Summary

You will have healthy motivation when (1) you have good reasons to do something you cherish doing; (2) these reasons are based on values and/or principles that are important to you, positive and life-enhancing; (3) you are not too preoccupied with striving towards more basic goals. While it may help you in your motivation if you also 'feel like' taking the required action, having such 'feeling' is ancillary to the presence of value-based reasons. To remind yourself of all these points when you are strongly tempted not to work towards your long-term goals and to make the decision to work towards them is an indication of inner strength.

In the next chapter, I will show you how to develop inner strength in the area of self-discipline.

3

How to discipline yourself

Introduction

To discipline yourself to reach important self-determined goals involves quite a bit of inner strength, and it is to this subject I now turn.

In my view, you are self-disciplined (1) when you have decided to work towards longer-term goals to which you have chosen to commit yourself and to forgo shorter-term goals that are obstacles to achieving these former goals *and* (2) when you act on this decision. When you are self-disciplined you acknowledge that there is a part of you that wishes to satisfy these shorter-term goals, but you are able to stand back and choose to pursue what is in your own best interests.

Self-discipline involves five components:

1 *Improvement* You have longer-term goals to which you have chosen to commit yourself.
2 *The long-term self* There is a part of you that has decided to work towards longer-term goals and that takes action in the service of these goals.
3 *The short-term self* There is also a part of you that wishes to satisfy these shorter-term goals.
4 *The executive self* There is yet another part of you that is able to stand back and choose to pursue what is in your own best interests.
5 *Obstacles* Developing self-discipline is rarely a smooth process and you will be faced with many obstacles to becoming more self-disciplined along the way.

I will presently discuss these five components in greater detail, but before I do let me distinguish between two different types of self-discipline.

Two forms of self-discipline

Let's imagine that you are overweight and your doctor strongly recommends that you lose weight. The factors that have probably contributed to you putting on weight are snacking on high-calorie food between meals and lack of exercise. Your doctor suggests two things to you: (1) cutting out snacking between meals and (2) taking exercise. Now these two suggestions illustrate the two different forms of self-discipline. The first – cutting out snacking between meals – involves you *not* doing something. I call this form of self-discipline 'refraining-based self-discipline' because it involves you refraining from taking action (in this case, not eating high-calorie snacks). The second form of self-discipline involves you doing something. I call this form of self-discipline 'action-based self-discipline' because it involves you in taking action (in this case, taking exercise).

Refraining-based self-discipline often involves you not doing something that you find pleasurable in the moment. Thus, in our example, you find eating high-calorie snacks pleasurable. As such, in order to develop this form of self-discipline, you need to develop ways of dealing effectively with temptation. By contrast, action-based self-discipline often involves you doing something that you find aversive in the moment. Thus, in our example, you find the process of moving from a comfortable state (e.g. sitting in an armchair when you are relaxed or tired) to an uncomfortable state (e.g. getting up and driving to the gym) aversive. As such, in order to develop this form of self-discipline, you need to deal effectively with discomfort.

Having distinguished between the two major forms of self-discipline, let me now discuss the five components of self-discipline in greater detail.

Improvement

Who defines your long-term goals?

As I pointed out in Chapter 2, if your longer-term self-discipline goals are truly your own, then, all things being equal, you are more likely to do the work to achieve them than if your goals have been introjected (i.e. accepted uncritically from another source) or suggested by someone else (e.g. a spouse or a parent). It follows, therefore, that you are more likely to initiate and sustain self-discipline action if your long-term goals are freely chosen.

Let's apply this principle to the scenario I introduced above, where your doctor advised you to lose weight by stopping unhealthy snacking between meals and by taking exercise. If you disagree with your doctor that you need to lose weight then you will not be defining your own long-term goals, and thus you will be unlikely to work towards them. However, if you agree with your doctor, then his or her suggested goals will become your own, and you will increase the chances that you will work towards achieving them, particularly if you also agree with the means of achieving your goals suggested by your doctor.

Making a commitment to seek improvement

As I have just mentioned, it is important that you freely choose your long-term self-discipline goals. Additionally, you increase the chances of initiating and sustaining self-disciplined behaviour if you make a commitment to achieve your goals. Making a commitment involves promising yourself that you are going to work towards your goals, and it also means that you are going to make this a priority. Some people benefit from making this commitment public, but others don't. Thus, you may benefit from telling other people that you have decided to lose weight or you may not.

As I implied above, different people make commitments to themselves in different ways. The important point here is that when you have decided to make a commitment to self-discipline goals you make this commitment in a way that is going to maximize your chances of acting on it and sustaining that action.

Implementing your commitment

When you are making a commitment to work towards your self-discipline goals, unless you implement your commitment and keep doing so, then you will be unlikely to achieve these goals. Implementation here means two things. It means taking action when you need to achieve your goals (e.g. by going to the gym to do the necessary exercise to help you lose weight) and it also means refraining from taking action when doing so also helps you to achieve your goals (e.g. by refraining from eating unhealthy snacks when you are tempted to).

Achievement vs maintenance

When you have achieved your self-discipline goals, then this is a matter of celebration. However, this is only half the story. For you need to continue to implement your commitment if you are to maintain your gains. The famous American writer Mark Twain summed up the difference between achieving self-discipline goals and maintaining them when he said, 'Giving up smoking is easy. I've done it hundreds of times.'

In some ways, maintaining your self-disciplined behaviour once you have achieved your goals is more difficult than achieving them in the first place. In addition, you need to respond constructively to lapses along the path to self-discipline and also to those occasions when you relapse. I will discuss these topics in Chapter 8.

The three selves

Sigmund Freud was renowned for the idea that humans have different parts of themselves that may work together or be in conflict with one another. In REBT, with respect to the area of self-discipline, I argue similarly that there are three parts of ourselves that need to be considered: (1) the long-term self; (2) the short-term self; and (3) the executive self.

The long-term self

As its name implies, your long-term self is concerned with your long-term health and development. It is not at all concerned with you seeking short-term pleasure or the short-term relief of immediate discomfort.

The short-term self

Your short-term self is concerned with satisfying your basic instincts. It is not at all concerned with your longer-term healthy interests. As noted above, your short-term self is not only concerned with pleasure, it is also concerned with the relief of pain and discomfort in their broadest sense.

The executive self

This next component of self-discipline is what I call the executive self. This is the part of you that mediates between the long-term and short-term selves. It helps to ensure that you have a healthy balance in life between pursuing your longer-term goals and satisfying your shorter-term goals.

Obstacles: what they are and how to address them effectively

The path towards self-discipline is filled with obstacles that need to be addressed and overcome. In this section, I will deal with three classes of obstacles and how to address them effectively: those that

- prevent you from taking self-disciplined action;
- lead you to take self-undisciplined action;
- encourage you to over-engage in your long-term goals.

Rigid beliefs about pre-action conditions: the biggest obstacle that prevents you from taking self-disciplined action

The biggest block to implementing your commitment to your longer-term self-discipline goals that involve you taking action concerns the conditions you believe have to exist before you take such action. In reality, while these conditions may be desirable they certainly don't have to exist before you take action towards your self-discipline goals, as we saw in Chapter 1.

In Table 3.1, I provide a list of such common conditions. For each condition, I list the rigid belief and provide the flexible alternative to this belief. It is important that you do the following if you want to free yourself from the constraints of these rigid beliefs:

- Identify the existence of such a rigid belief.
- Question it and respond to it with its flexible alternative.
- Take action while holding the flexible belief when the condition is not present.
- Accept that taking action in the absence of the desired condition goes against the comfortable grain.

Table 3.1 Rigid beliefs about the conditions that people insist must exist before they take action and their flexible belief alternatives

Condition	Rigid belief	Flexible belief
Motivation	'I have to be motivated to take action before I do so'	'It would be nice if I was motivated to take action before I do so, but that is not a necessary condition. I can take action even though I am not motivated if doing so will help me to achieve my longer-term goals'

Condition	Rigid belief	Flexible belief
Anxiety or pressure	'I have to feel anxious or under pressure before I take action'	'I don't have to feel anxious or under pressure before I take action. I can take action even though I am not anxious or under pressure'
Confidence	'I need to feel confident before I take action'	'It would be good if I felt confident before I took action, but I do not need this feeling in order to act'
Competence	'I must be competent at doing what I need to do before taking action'	'It would be good if I were competent at doing what I need to before taking action, but I do not need such competence in order to act'
Certainty	'I have to know what will happen if I take action before doing so'	'While it might be nice to know what will happen if I take action before doing so, I don't need such certainty in order to act'
External control	'I have to be in control of my environment before I take action'	'It may be good to be in control of my environment before I take action, but I do not need such control in order to act'
Self-control	'I must be in control of myself before I take action'	'It would be preferable if I were in control of myself before I took action, but this is not a necessary pre-condition for action'
Full comprehension	'I must understand everything concerning taking action before I do so'	'It would be good to understand everything concerning taking action before I do so, but I do not need full comprehension in order to act'
Comfort	'I must be comfortable before I take action'	'It would be desirable if I were comfortable before I took action, but I don't need such comfort in order to act'
Favourable external conditions	'Favourable external conditions must be present before I take action'	'I would like favourable external conditions to exist before I take action, but they don't need to. I can take action whether these conditions are favourable or not'

Here is the example of Max, who used the four points listed above.

Max wanted to write a dictionary of chemical terms, but was far too preoccupied with the best way to organize the material. Using the points above, Max identified that he held the following rigid belief that prevented him from working on his dictionary: 'I must know the best way to organize my dictionary before I start work on it.' Then Max responded to this rigid belief thus: 'While it would be great if I did know the best way of organizing my dictionary before I start work on it, this is only a desirable condition and not a necessary one. Since I am only likely to know the best way of organizing the material after I have started work on it, it would be in my best interest to start work on it now and discover the best way of organizing the material later.' With this belief in mind, Max started work on his dictionary even though he was uncomfortable about not knowing the best way of organizing it. Much later, he found the best way of structuring the work, and since he had written many of the entries it was not difficult for him to rewrite these to conform to his structure. If Max had waited to discover the best way of organizing his dictionary – i.e. if he had acted on his rigid belief – he would still not have started it!

Rigid beliefs about urges: the biggest obstacle that prevents you refraining from taking self-undisciplined action

In refraining-based self-discipline, you are called upon to deal with urges to engage in immediate pleasurable activities which go counter to the pursuit of your self-discipline goals. In biblical terms, your task in this area is to 'yield not to temptation' unless doing so has been incorporated into your overall self-discipline plan (e.g. having a planned bar of chocolate as part of a calorie-controlled diet). However, in this section I will assume that acting on your urges is not part of such a plan.

In order to deal with an urge, you need to understand what it is. An urge is a strong, often viscerally based tendency that you experience to engage in a pleasurable activity or rid yourself of a negative state. These go together in this sense. If you refrain from engaging in a pleasurable activity, you will probably experience some form of discomfort which you may be tempted to get rid of by engaging in the very same activity!

If you hold a rigid belief about experiencing such urges (such as 'If I feel like eating the cream cake then I have to do so' or 'I must get rid of discomfort as soon as I begin to experience it') then you will give in to temptation or act on your urges and thus set yourself back along the path towards self-discipline. As you might expect, developing ways of acting that are consistent with flexible alternatives to these rigid beliefs forms a central part of dealing effectively with such urges.

Coping with urges

Here are the steps that you need to take in order to deal effectively with such urges.

Acknowledge that you are experiencing an urge If you don't acknowledge that you are experiencing an urge, then you are likely to act on it. So you need to admit that you are tempted to do something that it is not in your long-term interests to do. It may help you to know where in your body you experience your urge. Some people feel it in their stomach, some feel restless, while for others the urge involves salivation. Once you have identified this, it may help you to say to yourself that you are experiencing an urge.

Acknowledge that you do not have to act on your urge immediately This step is particularly important in that it involves you rehearsing the rational belief that you don't have to act on the urge even though you want to. Breaking what might be called the urge–action fusion is very important in coping with urges.

Recognize that you have a choice: to act on the urge or not Once you have shown yourself that you don't have to act on your urge, you are then in a position to recognize that you can choose whether to act on your urge or to refrain from doing so. As I noted earlier, self-discipline does not just involve you acting in accord with your long-term interests; rather, it involves paying attention to these interests while ensuring that you also meet some of your short-term goals. Thus, you may choose to act on your urge if doing so does not interfere with you developing self-discipline. Having said this, it is important that you are honest with yourself and guard against using rationalizations to justify choosing to act on an urge when doing so is actually against your long-term interests.

Remind yourself of the positive reasons for refraining from acting on the urges and the negative reasons for acting on them If you have chosen to refrain from acting on your urge or you are still debating whether or not to do so, then you may benefit from reviewing the reasons why it is in your interests to refrain from acting on your urge and why it is not in your interests to act on the urge.

Respond to any 'positive' reasons for acting on your urge and to any 'negative' reasons against refraining from doing so While reviewing the pros and cons of acting on your urge and of refraining from doing so, you may discover pros for acting on them and cons against refraining from doing so. If you do, it is important that you respond to such reasons so that you neutralize their effect on your behaviour or your decision-making.

Take purposive action even though you are experiencing the urge If you have decided to refrain from acting on your urge then it is important that you get on with what you would be doing if you did not experience an urge. Do so even though you experience the urge. If you do this, then you will discover that the intensity of your urge will initially increase since you are not satisfying it, but then it will decrease.

Tilly wanted to give up smoking for health reasons. She used the steps outlined above in the following ways:

- She recognized that she had an urge to smoke whenever she had a coffee break. She recognized this from her restless hands.
- She told herself that while she wanted a cigarette at that moment she did not have to act on that urge.
- Tilly reminded herself that she had a choice. She could go with her urge or go against it.
- Tilly briefly reminded herself that the reason she wanted to give up smoking was to stop getting chest infections and to reduce the chances of getting lung cancer. She also reminded herself that if she smoked she would smell 'like an ashtray'.
- In doing this she recognized that she felt 'cool' while she smoked. She asked herself whether having this transitory feeling was worth jeopardizing her health for and she concluded that it wasn't. So she told herself that while it was nice to feel cool, she did not have to have this feeling.
- She decided to keep her cigarettes in her handbag and not smoke.

Rigid beliefs about pursuing your long-term goals: the biggest obstacle to balanced living

Some people are so adept at resisting the temptation to meet their short-term goals and pursuing their long-term goals that they become rigid about doing so. As a result they do not lead a balanced life, and are so compulsive about working to achieve their long-term goals that they derive little pleasure in life. Their long-term self is in total control and they not only quash their short-term self, they also do not listen to their executive self which, if you recall, is charged with the task of mediating between their short-term self and their long-term self. If this applies to you, then you need to do the following:

- Recognize the advantages of a balanced approach of meeting some of your short-term goals while staying on track on the path towards your long-term goals, and accept that only pursuing your long-term goals will lead you to experience burnout.

- Acknowledge that you feel uncomfortable about meeting your short-term goals when you could be pursuing your long-term goals.
- Show yourself that you don't always have to pursue your long-term goals and can tolerate the discomfort of pursuing your short-term goals, and that it is worthwhile doing so.
- Remind yourself that you are not being undisciplined if you take a balanced approach to your short-term and long-term goals.
- Plan to pursue your short-term goals and actually do so.

Amir was studying medicine, and it was so important to him that he qualify as a doctor that he refused to spend any time away from his studies even though he liked socializing and engaging in various sports activities. Amir's tutor was concerned about him and urged him to have more balance in his life. After much thought, Amir agreed. He decided to spend one weekday evening doing sports and one evening at the weekend socializing. He reminded himself of the reasons for engaging in these activities and of the fact that he did not always have to study. At the beginning he forced himself to go out at the appointed times even though he felt uncomfortable doing so. He tolerated this discomfort and went out. After a few weeks, Amir saw for himself the benefits of a balanced approach to life: he realized that taking time away from his studies refreshed him and would help him in the longer term to qualify as a doctor, rendering him less vulnerable to burnout. At that point engaging in his short-term goals was a pleasure and not a chore.

Summary

Self-discipline involves you being clear about your long-term self-discipline goals, committing yourself to pursuing them and taking action to do so. However, over the long haul you are more likely to be self-disciplined if you also plan to meet some of your short-term goals. In action-based self-discipline you need to identify any conditions you believe must be in place before you take action, showing yourself that however desirable they may be, these pre-action conditions don't have to exist and that you can take action in their absence. In refraining-based self-discipline, you need to cope with temptation to engage in the short-term pleasurable or discomfort-removing activity by showing yourself that you don't have to act on these urges. In this way you can develop self-discipline-based inner strength.

In the following chapter, I will consider the topic of resilience.

4

How to become more resilient

Introduction

Resilience is a specific form of inner strength which involves you responding healthily to some kind of adversity. However, in order to become more resilient it is important that you understand the nature of resilience. Unfortunately, resilience is often a misunderstood concept. Thus, it is commonly seen to involve the following:

1 You are in a state of equilibrium.
2 You experience some kind of disruption to this existing state (e.g. a setback).
3 You make a quick and relatively smooth return to the state that existed before the disruption occurred.

There are a number of problems with this view, of which the most serious are:

- It does not allow for the fact that the state you were in before the disruption may have been unhealthy.
- It implies that your return to the same state of equilibrium that existed before the negative event happened is a defining feature of resilience.
- It expounds the myth of you quickly bouncing back.
- It does not consider that resilience often involves you in feeling emotional pain and struggle.
- It overlooks what I call the 'resilience behaviour ratio'. Resilience, in my view, can be best seen as representing a ratio of healthy and unhealthy behaviour. The more healthily you behave in the face of adversity, the greater resilience you

are demonstrating. Note then that resilience allows for the fact that, at times, you may well lose the struggle and act in short-term protective but resilience-defeating ways. However, as long as your ratio is in credit (greater healthy to unhealthy behaviour) then you are acting resiliently in the face of adversity. Your goal then becomes to develop greater resilience and increase your resilience behaviour ratio. The common view of resilience does not allow for the existence of such a ratio.

Resilience using RECBT's Situational ABC framework

In Chapter 1, I discussed the major rational beliefs that underpin inner strength and contrasted these with the irrational beliefs that underpin psychological disturbance. I will refer to these beliefs as I outline RECBT's Situational ABC framework which, in my view, is a better way of understanding what happens when you encounter an adversity, flounder and then develop a more resilient response. By understanding this process, you can learn to become more resilient. Let me outline the components of the Situational ABC framework, and in doing so I will assume that you are facing some kind of adversity.

Situation

The situation is the context in which your response occurs. It is best seen as descriptive in nature and can be reliably described by a group of objective observers.

'A' = activating event

An activating event (or 'A') is the aspect of the situation to which you are responding. An 'A' can be an actual event within the larger situation or an inference that you make about the situation. An inference is an interpretation of the situation that goes beyond the data at hand. It may be correct or incorrect, but you need to test it against the available data.

'B' = beliefs

The common view of resilience that I have presented only refers to events that occur at 'A' (i.e. a setback) or responses that occur at 'C' (i.e. quick recovery) – see below. It does not refer to what I consider to be the most important factor in resilience. This is 'B', the beliefs you hold about the adversities, which determine whether you respond resiliently to the adversities or not. This is ultimately why the common view of resilience is problematic. It ignores what I call the heart of resilience – which is your belief system.

As we saw earlier in this book, beliefs can be held about yourself, others and the world. Resilience-based beliefs tend to be flexible and non-extreme in nature while beliefs that get in the way of resilient responding are rigid and extreme in nature.

'C' = consequences

As I said earlier, 'C' factors are the responses that you make to events at 'A' that are mediated by your beliefs at 'B'. There are three major consequences of 'B' that are particularly relevant to an understanding of resilience. These are emotions (emotional consequences), behaviour (behavioural consequences) and thinking (thinking consequences).

Emotions

Emotions can either be positive or negative in tone, or you may lack emotion.

Resilience is not marked by an absence of emotion

A common misconception of resilience is that it involves Stoicism, a response to adversity characterized by strength and lacking emotion. Nothing can be further from the truth. Indeed, absence of emotion is often a sign that you have not properly digested what has happened to you and bodes poorly for future resilience. The only true way that you can have an unemotional response to what has happened to you is when you genuinely care nothing about what has occurred. Consider the situation where you look outside your window and notice that a car has drawn up opposite your house. If you have no emotions about this fact it is because it holds no significance to you whatsoever. It is a neutral event. As I argued above, adversities are negative in nature, and thus to respond to them without emotion is not healthy and is not a good example of resilience.

Resilience is not marked by positive emotion

When you respond resiliently to adversity you do not have a positive emotion. In order to have a positive emotion about adversity you would have to believe that it is good that the adversity happened, which is, as you can see, quite ludicrous.

Resilience is marked by negative emotion

As an adversity is a negative event, it is healthy to experience a negative emotion in response. Now, as we saw in Chapter 1, negative emotions can be healthy or unhealthy. When they are healthy they stem from rational beliefs, and when they are unhealthy they stem from irrational beliefs. Since resilience is based on rational beliefs, it therefore follows that a resilient response to an adversity is marked by a healthy negative emotion.

Behaviour

In this section, I will consider behavioural responses to adversity. I would argue that unless you put your resilient attitudes into practice you cannot truly be said to be demonstrating resilience. Acting resiliently is literally resilience in action!

Action tendencies and overt behaviour

Any behaviour can be divided into a tendency to act and an overt action. This is a very important distinction since resilience often involves (1) refraining from doing what you 'feel like' doing and (2) doing what you don't 'feel like' doing.

This difference between an action tendency and an overt behaviour is an important one. A realistic view of resilience states that resilience is based more on a person not converting a self-defeating action tendency into overt behaviour than it is on the absence of this action tendency.

Thinking

When thinking is the product of your beliefs about an adversity your 'subsequent thinking', as I call it, is likely to be inferential in nature. When it stems from flexible rational beliefs this subsequent thinking tends to be balanced and realistic in nature, while when it stems from rigid irrational beliefs it tends to be heavily skewed to the negative and highly distorted in nature. Since resilience involves struggle, you may experience both types of subsequent thinking as you swing from holding flexible beliefs to holding rigid beliefs and back again, until you eventually hold the former rather than the latter.

Dryden's definition of resilience

Based on all the issues that I have discussed in this chapter, I will now put forward my own working definition of resilience. I will first present my view and then discuss its component parts.

What is resilience?

Resilience comprises a set of flexible and cognitive, behavioural and emotional responses to acute or chronic adversities that can be unusual or commonplace. These responses can be learned and are within the grasp of everyone. While many factors affect the development of resilience, the most important one is the belief that you hold about the adversity. Therefore, belief is the heart of resilience.

Resilience, as commonly understood, refers to 'bouncing back' from difficult experiences. A more detailed and realistic understanding of resilience involves you frequently experiencing pain and struggle while 'coming back' rather than 'bouncing back' from misfortune. This experience of pain and struggle does not stop you from working to change those adversities that can be changed and from adjusting constructively to those that cannot be changed. Nor does the experience of pain and struggle stop you from moving towards your goals, however slowly, or pursuing what is important to you. This forward movement is a defining feature of resilience. As such, resilience does not restore the status quo in your life before the adversity occurred. Rather, what you have learned changes you for the better and helps you to become more acutely aware of what is important in your life and, as I have said, it encourages you to pursue it.

While resilience is the response of you as an individual, its development can be facilitated or impaired by the context in which you live, such as, respectively, having supportive friends or experiencing violent abuse from your partner, and thus is best understood within this context.

Here are the components of my view of resilience:

Resilience comprises a set of flexible cognitive, behavioural and emotional responses

There is nothing mystical about resilience. It can be explained with reference to psychological processes – cognitive (or thinking), emotional and behavioural – that are flexible in nature.

Resilience can occur in response to acute or chronic adversities that can be unusual or commonplace

It is a popular view of resilience that it mainly occurs in response to dramatic, catastrophic events. Common discussions of resilience specifically mention people's responses to the events that happened in the USA on September 11th, 2001. Newspaper accounts of resilience more often than not focus on resilience in the face of unusual events, both acute (i.e. dramatic events that are time-bound, like 9/11 or a tsunami) and chronic (i.e. long-lasting events, like the case of Elisabeth Fritzl, the Austrian girl who was held captive for many years).

While it is true that people can and often do respond resiliently to unusual acute or chronic adversities, it is very important not to overlook resilience in the face of adversities that are more commonplace, since this is the experience of most of us.

These responses can be learned and are within the grasp of everyone

These are two very important points. First, it is encouraging for people to discover that they can *learn* to become resilient, that resilience is not just the province of those fortunate enough to be born with hardy genes. While people are born with different temperaments, with some people naturally responding in a more resilient way to adversities than others, everyone can learn to become more resilient. Learning resilience means practice, so while reading a book on how to become more resilient, for example, can be the first step along the path to greater resilience, it is important that you recognize that you need to put into practice what you read in such a book if you are truly to learn it.

Belief is the heart of resilience

The well-known Stoic philosopher Epictetus once famously said that people are disturbed not by events but by their views of events. I think that these 'views' are best seen as representing people's beliefs and thus I would say that a person's resilient response at 'C' (in the ABC framework discussed above) to adversities at 'A' is dependent on his or her belief at 'B'.

Resilience does not mean 'bouncing back' from difficult experiences. Rather, it involves you experiencing pain and struggle as you come back from misfortune

I have mentioned a number of times in this chapter that a popular conception of resilience is that it involves the person 'bouncing back' from adversity. The concept of 'bouncing back' conjures up an image of a quick and easy return to a previous state that is to be found in the common view of resilience. I prefer to talk of 'coming back' from misfortune, which can and often does involve pain and struggle, and in a way that involves learning from the experience rather than returning to the previous pre-adversity state. As I said in my definition: '. . . what you have learned changes you for the better and helps you to become more acutely aware of what is important in your life and . . . encourages you to pursue it'.

Moving forward is a defining feature of resilience

While I stress that emotional pain and struggle very frequently accompanies resilience, I also stress that this pain and struggle does not stop you from pursuing your goals and addressing the obstacles that might interfere with goal achievement. Hence, resilience helps you to move forward and is one of its defining features.

Resilience changes you for the better

I stress that, rather than returning you to the state you were in before the adversity occurred, resilience changes you for the better and helps you to become more aware of what your life's goals are and the importance of actively pursuing them.

Resilience is best understood within the context in which it occurs

While it is true that resilience is demonstrated by individuals, it is also true that the context in which it occurs is important too, and therefore if you wish to develop resilience you need to pay attention to contextual factors (the external) as well as factors within yourself (the internal).

My definition of resilience should, however, best be regarded as a work in progress rather than fixed in stone since, like resilience itself, a good definition of resilience should be flexible and promote change.

Case examples

Let me show how two people used the principles described in this chapter to respond resiliently to adversity.

Robert was a secondary school teacher who was devoted to his job, so much so that he worked far longer than his contracted hours. In addition, he volunteered to organize and run after-school sports activities. He was then accused by one of his pupils of indecent behaviour and he was suspended on full pay pending an inquiry and police investigation.

Initially, Robert was devastated. He felt unhealthily angry that his school did not support him and very hurt that he could be accused of such a thing, given all he had done for the children. Robert took a few days' break with his wife and rethought the situation. He realized that while his school could have done more to support him they did not have to do that and he could see that they were following a protocol. He also came to see that just because he gave so much to the children this did not mean that he was immune from an accusation of sexual abuse and sadly he did not have to be so immune. As he worked towards this rational resilience belief, Robert was still shaken, but with his wife's support and faith in him he went back home and told people what was happening to him. He also started to think about his life in a wider context and realized that he had neglected his wife and family and that he was giving far too much of himself to school.

The police decided that he had no case to answer and the school enquiry exonerated him so he was reinstated. However, the Robert who went back to school was different from the Robert who gave so much of his time and energy to the school and its children prior to the accusation. While he was still committed to the school, he stopped organizing the after-hours school activities and instead spent this time with his wife and his own children. His family blossomed as a result. He also started to be more circumspect about being alone with children in situations in which he felt vulnerable.

Months later, Robert had moved on with his life, still disappointed that his school had not shown him emotional support but pleased that this situation had provided him with an opportunity to rethink important life priorities.

Jackie, a 24-year-old woman, was run over by a motorcyclist as she was crossing the road, and after extensive surgery she had to have her left leg amputated. When she discovered this she was understandably distressed, but when she was discharged from hospital she went into a severe depression and started drinking heavily. Thinking this was a phase, at first her parents did not urge her to seek help, but after a month, as her alcohol consumption increased and her depression deepened, they pressed her to see a therapist, something she reluctantly agreed to do.

Initially, Jackie did not engage in therapy but she did agree to stop drinking. This helped her to see that she was adding needless suffering to her personal loss. Slowly, Jackie began to see that she was taking this tragedy and demanding that it absolutely should not have happened to her. As a result she concluded that her life was over and she might as well be dead. With her therapist's help, Jackie challenged this irrational belief and came to accept that while what had happened to her was tragic, it did not mean the end of her life and she could still live a meaningful and happy life even though she had lost her leg. She also accepted the bitter pill that she was not immune from such tragedy and nor did she have to be. This helped her to accept that she had a choice: to wallow in self-pity and go back to drinking or to accept the grim reality of her loss and get on with life. Fortunately she chose the latter.

Consequently, when the time was right medically she was fitted with a prosthesis and began the arduous journey of learning to walk again with her artificial limb. She was inspired in this by the stories of Douglas Bader (who lost both legs in the Second World War) and Heather Mills (the model and disability campaigner) who both learned to walk again after losing a limb. After much physical and mental struggle she too learned to walk again but, as she said herself, she also learned something more valuable. She learned that she had great reserves of inner strength which she had never known she had, and decided that she was going to use this strength to help young people to cope with similar injuries and to go to university to study for a degree, neither of which she had ever even considered when she had two legs.

The stories of Robert and Jackie clearly show that true resilience does not involve bouncing back to a pre-disruptive state. It involves something far more meaningful than that. It involves great personal struggle, re-evaluation of one's belief system and a commitment to a more meaningful life.

Summary

In this chapter, I have considered two views of resilience: one which involves bouncing back from adversity to a pre-disruptive state, and the other which regards resilience as involving pain and struggle but where a person learns something important from the struggle and is enriched by it. I argued that the latter is best regarded as true resilience and is underpinned by the set of rational beliefs that I discussed in Chapter 1 as the foundations of inner strength. In the next chapter, I will consider the inner strength involved in standing up for what you believe in when doing so may involve a personal cost.

5

How to stand up for what you believe in

Introduction

As I discussed in Chapter 1, this book is based on Rational-Emotive Cognitive Behavioural Therapy (RECBT). I argued there that this name shows that the approach is placed within the Cognitive Behavioural Therapy (CBT) tradition and that its distinctive features are synonymous with an approach known as Rational Emotive Behavioural Therapy (REBT) which was originated in 1955 by Dr Albert Ellis (1913–2007). Had it not been for the inner strength shown by Dr Ellis it is very unlikely that I would have written this book. So let me tell you a little of the struggles that Dr Ellis had to contend with in promulgating his ideas, for the inner strength that he demonstrated is what this chapter is all about.

Dr Ellis was originally trained in psychoanalysis, but always doubted its effectiveness and efficiency. After experimenting with the range of therapeutic approaches of the time, Ellis originated his own approach, which he called 'Rational Therapy'. This emphasized the role that irrational ideas played in the development and maintenance of emotional problems. Ellis argued that a direct attack on these ideas was warranted and that people also needed to act against these ideas and in line with alternative rational ideas. Ellis was keen to make his ideas widely known, and to that end he published his ideas in professional journals and popular magazines and sent interested practitioners reel-to-reel recordings of his therapy sessions with patients using Rational Therapy.

Initially he attracted a small group of followers, but he received far more criticism than praise in the professional field of psychotherapy, dominated as it was by practitioners of psychoanalytic therapy and client-centred therapy. But Ellis was not distracted from his purpose by these criticisms. He stood up for what he believed in and wrote vigorous rebuttals of these criticisms as part of trying to ensure that his views were accurately represented in the field.

It would have been very easy for Ellis to crumble under the relentless stream of criticism of his views and even in the face of personal attacks. But he didn't crumble or crack. He persisted with making his views known, and gradually these views became more widely understood and accepted. Indeed, Dr Ellis is generally regarded as one of the founders of the CBT tradition in psychotherapy, a tradition which is still receiving criticism but largely because it is seen as too influential in the field of psychotherapy!

Understanding the process that enabled Dr Ellis to continue to stand up for what he believed in in the face of such personal and professional vilification will help you to develop the inner strength to stand up for what you believe in in the face of similar negativity.

Learning from the experience of Dr Ellis

I knew Dr Ellis personally for about 25 years and can attest to the dimensions of inner strength that helped him to withstand the slings and arrows of outrageous fortune in the early years of REBT's development

It seems to me that the following dimensions of inner strength were important in helping Dr Ellis to stand up and continue to stand up for what he believed in.

Clarity of conviction

I mentioned in Chapter 2 that one of the best ways of motivating yourself is knowing the reasons it is important for you to do something. Such self-motivation is particularly strong if these reasons are underpinned by important values or principles that you can keep in mind, particularly when the going gets tough.

Dr Ellis was passionately concerned with helping people to solve their emotional problems. In addition, he believed strongly in the principles of efficiency and self-help, and saw in the early 1950s that the extant forms of therapeutic help were inefficient (i.e. very time-consuming) and did not encourage people to help themselves. His newly developing approach recommended that people suffering emotional problems focus directly on the irrational ideas that underpinned these problems and develop an alternative set of rational ideas instead. From his standpoint it was more efficient and put greater emphasis on self-help than did psychoanalytic and client-centred approaches.

Thus, Dr Ellis had a clear idea of why he was doing what he was doing, and his activity was based on principles that he held very dear.

A healthy response to disapproval

Dr Ellis received a great deal of disapproval when he first presented his ideas about Rational Therapy in the 1950s. Now, Dr Ellis, like most other humans, preferred to receive approval rather than disapproval, for approval is good in itself and it would have smoothed the way for him to have his ideas accepted by the therapeutic community. The fact that he continued to promulgate his ideas in the face of disapproval means that his desire for approval did not stop him, even though he did not get his desire met.

As I made clear in Chapter 1, when we don't get what we want in life, it is our beliefs about these unmet desires that is crucial in determining our emotional and behavioural response to this situation. When we hold a flexible belief we respond healthily to this situation, but when our belief is rigid then our response is unhealthy.

It is clear from this that Dr Ellis's belief about disapproval was flexible (i.e. 'I would prefer to avoid disapproval, but I don't have to do so'). This flexible belief helped him to weigh his desire to avoid disapproval against his desire to bring his ideas to the attention of the professional community and to the public, and in Ellis's case the latter desire was much stronger than the former. Consequently, he decided to continue his promulgation efforts rather than stay quiet and avoid disapproval. On the other hand, if his belief about disapproval had been rigid (i.e. 'I must avoid disapproval'), then he would have stopped promulgating his ideas since that would have been the way he could have avoided disapproval. Thus, holding flexible beliefs about disapproval is a hallmark of inner strength.

Self-acceptance in the face of criticism

Since the mid-1950s, Dr Ellis's ideas have received much criticism from therapists of other traditions. He reacted to these criticisms with an open mind. Thus, when people claimed that the term 'Rational Therapy' implied that his approach neglected emotion, Ellis changed the name of his approach to 'Rational-Emotive Therapy' (RET). And later, when people claimed that RET neglected behaviour, Ellis again changed the name of his approach to 'Rational Emotive Behavioural Therapy' (REBT).

While Dr Ellis did not care for many of the criticisms that were made of his ideas, he did not base his self-esteem on whether his ideas were accepted or rejected. This enabled him to go forward with his work and the promulgation of what he truly believed. If Dr Ellis had based his self-esteem on his ideas being accepted, he would have modified them to get them accepted, even though this would have meant compromising his true convictions. As we will see, self-acceptance in the face of criticism is a feature of inner strength in many domains.

Healthy anger

Over the years, and especially at the beginning, Dr Ellis received very unfair criticism and personal attacks. While he was angry about this, his anger was generally healthy in nature. Thus, he did not believe: 'These people absolutely must not be so unfair in their criticisms and attacks. They are bad people for doing so and deserve to be punished.' Rather, he believed: 'I really don't like the fact that these people are unfairly criticizing and attacking me, but sadly and regretfully, there is no law decreeing that they must not do so. These are not bad people; rather, they are fallible people doing bad things.' If Dr Ellis's anger had been unhealthy, he would have become side-tracked into bitter fights with people he would have regarded as his enemies. Getting thus involved would have taken him away from further developing his ideas and disseminating them.

Fighting the good fight

Although Dr Ellis did not get involved in exchanges based on unhealthy anger, he was assiduous in responding to the serious criticisms that were made about his theory. He did so for a number of reasons. First, Dr Ellis enjoyed a vigorous debate. Second, responding to his critics gave him the opportunity to correct the misconceptions that they had about his approach. Third, responding to his critics gave Dr Ellis a further opportunity to promulgate his ideas to the profession.

Discomfort tolerance and persistence

If Dr Ellis had hoped for a quick favourable response to his ideas, he was sadly mistaken. Indeed, if he had demanded such a response from the professional community, then he would have given up when it became clear that such a response would not be forthcoming. However, he was realistic in his prediction that it would take quite a while and a lot of effort to have his ideas accepted by a sceptical field, if indeed his ideas would be accepted at all. While he may not have liked this grim reality, he accepted it and tolerated the discomfort of dealing with all the negativity that came his way. Tolerating such discomfort made it easier for Dr Ellis to persist in standing up for what he believed in.

How to stand up for what you believe in

Let me now generalize from Dr Ellis's example to help you see what you need to do to stand up for what you believe in.

Be clear with yourself about what you do believe in

There is a great line in the 1953 remake of *The Jazz Singer* that is relevant to the point I want to make here. It is this: 'Do whatever is in your heart. But first, know what is in your heart.' In this film, the son of the cantor (the person who sings the prayers in a synagogue) is torn between doing what he wants to do (sing in show business) and following the family tradition (succeeding his father as cantor in the synagogue, as all the men in his family have done for over two centuries). He wavers back and forth, and tries a few times to persuade himself that he really does want to be a cantor when it is clear that he does not want this. At those times he listens to the part of him that tells him what he should want rather than to the part of him that tells him what he truly wants.

How can you tell what you really believe in (i.e. what is in your heart)? For as the line above makes clear, if you don't know what is in your heart, then it is difficult to follow it. The best suggestion I have for you is this: if the people who oppose you in what you believe were to suddenly drop their opposition and support you, would their change of heart make it easier for you to know what is in your heart? If the answer is yes, then this is what you truly believe in. Let me apply this to the cantor's son. Suppose his father had said to him: 'Son, you know I have been wrong to try to encourage you to follow the family tradition. I really want you to do what you want to do and I will support you 100 per cent in your decision.' What would his son have done? As the film shows, he would have expressed his singing talents in show business rather than in the synagogue and would have experienced no conflict in doing so.

So if you experience a conflict between what you think you believe in and what you should believe in, I suggest you use this method to help you discover what is truly in your heart.

Identify and assess the obstacles to you standing up for what you believe in

Once you have identified what it is that you truly believe in, then it would be easy for you to stand up for this if there were no obstacles to you doing so. Indeed, if this was the case then you would not need inner strength, since standing up under these very favourable conditions would be easy. It is when such obstacles do exist – or when you think they exist – that you are faced with a choice: do you stand up for what you believe in or not? The first step to dealing with these obstacles is to identify and assess them. A good way of doing this is to use the RECBT's Situational ABC framework. Let me demonstrate how to do this by discussing the case of Roy.

> Roy was a mature student doing a degree in politics and held right-wing political views. Most of the other students in his tutorial group were much younger and held left-wing political views. In the tutorial discussions most of the students discussed topics from their left-wing perspective, and Roy wanted to put his point of view but ended up not doing so.

Here is how Roy used the Situational ABC framework to identify and assess his obstacle to voicing his deeply held views in the tutorial.

Describe the situation ('Situation')

Here you describe the situation that you were in when you wanted to stand up for what you believe in but didn't.

> Roy: 'I was in a tutorial with six other students and the tutor, all of whom were expressing left-wing views on the tutorial topic. I wanted to express my views but didn't.'

Identify the major emotion that stopped you from standing up for what you believe in ('C')

> Roy: Anxiety

Identify what you were most disturbed about in the situation you were in ('A') and assume temporarily that 'A' is true

> Roy: 'I was most anxious about them ridiculing me if I expressed my right-wing views. I am going to assume temporarily that they ridicule me.'

Identify your main rigid and extreme beliefs about 'A' that accounted for your disturbance and failure to stand up for what you believe in at 'C'

> Roy: 'They must not ridicule me, and if they do it proves that I am useless.'

Major obstacles to standing up for what you believe in

The main emotion that people experience that accompanies their decision not to stand up for what they believe in is anxiety. Here is a list of such common anxieties:

- Fear of criticism
- Fear of disapproval
- Fear of ridicule
- Fear of retaliation
- Fear of being penalized
- Fear of conflict
- Fear of discomfort.

Set realistic goals

We know that your behavioural goal is to stand up for what you believe in, but it is important to set a realistic emotional goal, one that is a realistic response to the actual or predicted adversity at 'A' but one that enables you to stand up for what you believe in despite this adversity. In general the healthy alternative to anxiety is concern.

> Roy: 'I want to express my true political views in the tutorial and to feel concerned but not anxious about the prospect of being ridiculed for doing so.'

Question your beliefs

The purpose of questioning your beliefs is for you to recognize the irrationality of your irrational beliefs and the rationality of your alternative rational beliefs.

Develop rational beliefs

In order to do this you first need to develop rational alternatives to your irrational beliefs (see Chapter 1).

> Roy: 'My rational alternative belief is as follows: "I don't want them to ridicule me, but that does not mean that they must not do so. If they do, it does not prove that I am useless. I am a fallible human being who cannot be defined by others ridiculing my political views."'

How to question your beliefs

Now you can take both your irrational and rational beliefs and ask yourself which of these is true and which false, which is sensible and which illogical, and which is constructive and which unconstructive. It is important to provide reasons for your choice.

> Roy: 'It is true that I don't want my classmates to ridicule me, but it is also true that they don't have to meet my preferences. Also, my rational belief is sensible as both parts of the belief are non-rigid and thus logically connected with one another. Also, if I

really believe my rational belief, I will speak up for what I believe in, which is what I want to do.

'On the other hand, my irrational belief is false, for if it were true it would not be possible for my classmates to ridicule me. Also, it is not sensible for me to say that because I don't want them to ridicule me they must not do so. Finally, my irrational belief is unconstructive, for it would stop me from standing up for what I believe in.'

Act on your rational beliefs

The only way you will truly have conviction in your rational beliefs is if you act in ways that are consistent with them. In most cases, this involves you rehearsing your rational beliefs while standing up for what you believe in.

Roy resolved to voice his right-wing views at every tutorial. He first rehearsed his rational belief and reminded himself that while he would prefer his fellow students not to ridicule him, they do not have to do what he wants and that he can accept himself in the face of their ridicule. He then kept this rational belief in mind while voicing his right-wing views. He did this at every tutorial and in doing so lost his fear about standing up for what he believed in.

Be flexible and watch out for the 'no matter what' effect

RECBT notes that it is easy for people to make healthy ideas unhealthy by being rigid about them. In this chapter, I have been advocating the virtues of standing up for what you believe in, and in general this is a good thing for you to do. However, it is important that you watch out for signs that you are transforming your healthy preference concerning standing up for what you believe in into a rigid dogma. When you do so you believe that you must stand up for what you believe in no matter what. That is why I call this the 'no matter what' effect. If you find signs of this effect, it is important that you question your demands since they will probably get you into real trouble before long. This was the case with Maureen.

For most of her life, Maureen would agree with other people when they voiced views that were opposite to her own. When her boss at work offered her the opportunity to have ongoing sessions with a life coach, Maureen jumped at the chance for she knew that she was unhappy with her behaviour in this respect. Her life coach helped her to have the courage of her convictions and stand up for what she believed in whenever others voiced ideas that she disagreed with. So far, so good. However, Maureen became rigid about speaking her mind. She argued that because it was generally a good thing to stand up for what she believed in, she had to do it at every opportunity. She also held that because she had acquiesced with other people for much of her life, she absolutely must not do so again.

Mr Jones, her boss, liked the fact that Maureen now spoke up for what she believed in and, indeed, he was the one who encouraged her to seek life coaching to help her to do this. However, problems started for Maureen when Mr Jones left the company to be replaced by a new boss, Mr Green. Unlike Mr Jones, Mr Green did not encourage his staff to stand up for what they believed in. He had a more authoritarian style and discouraged staff from expressing their opinions when these contradicted his own. Maureen, however, was not to be denied and kept standing up for what she believed in, even though she could tell her boss was becoming impatient and cross with her for doing so.

The result of this clash was that Maureen was eventually fired from her job, a job she really loved. The reason for this was that she did not choose her moments to stand up for her convictions with her new boss. She felt compelled to do so at every opportunity, even when she did not really care that much for whatever it was she was standing up for.

This last point in Maureen's story is important. When you hold a rigid belief about standing up for what you believe in, you tend not to think about the consequences of doing so. Also, you tend not to discriminate between beliefs that are very important to you and are worth standing up for even in the face of adversity, and negative consequences and other beliefs that are perhaps not so important to you and are only worth standing up for when the conditions under which you are doing so are more favourable.

The flexible alternative to this rigid belief is as follows: 'It is important for me to stand up for what I believe in, but I do not always have to do so.' Holding such a flexible belief about standing up for what you believe in enables you to make subtle judgements about the pros and cons of doing so, and allows you to choose not to stand up for what you believe in when to do so would be counterproductive to you. If Maureen had held such a flexible belief it is likely that she would have held on to her job while she looked around for one which encouraged employees to express their deeply held views.

Summary

Standing up for what you believe in when you are facing obstacles to doing so often takes great inner strength. It involves dealing effectively with criticism, disapproval, ridicule, retaliation, being penalized, conflict and discomfort. Holding a set of rational beliefs about such adversities enables you to choose when to stand up for what you believe in and when not to. You can only do this when you are flexible and not rigid about such self-expression. In the next chapter, I will show you how you can deal effectively with family pressure.

6

How to deal effectively with family pressure

Introduction

Aaron was a 25-year-old man who was brought up in a traditional Jewish family. He went to synagogue every Sabbath and observed the main Jewish holy days and festivals, and some of the lesser ones as well. He was proud of his Jewish heritage, and as everyone in his immediate and extended family held the same beliefs and observed the same holy days and festivals, Aaron experienced very little, if any, conflict in matters to do with his religion. The only thing that was missing from Aaron's life was a 'nice Jewish girl' to complete the picture. Aaron was a newly qualified chartered accountant with a bright professional future ahead of him. He was a good-looking man and was heterosexual. Over the years he had met a number of suitable Jewish women and had dated a few, but nothing developed into the steady relationship that Aaron wanted for himself, a desire shared by all of his family. When it became clear that Aaron was having difficulty finding a suitable partner, close family members went into action looking for appropriate Jewish women to introduce to Aaron. He appreciated the help and was open to such introductions and going on the blind dates that were set up for him. He also went on JDate, an internet dating site exclusively for single Jewish people wishing to meet members of the opposite sex. But all this was to no avail. It was not that Aaron was too picky or had qualities that put women off. It was just that nothing developed beyond the third or fourth date.

Aaron loved the theatre and helped out at his local drama group. It was there that something happened that would change the course of his life. He was instantly drawn to Samantha, a 24-year-old woman who had just joined the drama group, and this attraction was mutual. They went out for a few drinks and spent hours in conversation, discovering that they had much in common. However, there was a fly in the ointment – Samantha was not Jewish. Aaron could see the dangers involved in beginning a relationship with Samantha and explained this to her. She was very disappointed but understood the risks involved in Aaron dating a non-Jewish woman. So they did not pursue their mutual attraction.

The trouble was, Aaron could not stop thinking of Samantha, and this was made worse by the fact that they saw one another at the drama group two evenings a week. Aaron decided that the best course of action was for him to join a different drama group. He did this, but it did not solve the problem. He could not get Samantha out of his mind.

Aaron was sad and miserable. He went through the motions of his life, and although his family members noticed the change in his mood he denied that anything was wrong. While he continued to date Jewish women his heart was no longer in the dating process and he only had single dates with these women.

Mike, Aaron's best friend, also noticed the change in him, but unlike Aaron's family members would not be fobbed off by his friend's protestations that there was nothing wrong. Mike continued to press Aaron until the latter broke down in tears and told Mike the whole story. Mike was also Jewish and knew what internal turmoil Aaron was going through, but he could see that Aaron really cared for Samantha. To Aaron's shock and surprise, he recommended that Aaron follow his heart, promising that he would support him in dealing with the enormous pressure both predicted Aaron would be under once his family discovered that he was going out with a non-Jewish woman.

Encouraged by Mike's response, Aaron contacted Samantha and they started going out. Soon they were inseparable. Aaron felt that at last he had found his soul mate, and when he disclosed his feelings to Samantha she told him that she felt the same. Once he heard this he resolved to tell his family. He predicted that their response would be highly unfavourable and he was right!

In the following sections I will discuss the different types of pressure Aaron experienced from his immediate and wider family and how he dealt with them using the principles presented in this book. As these pressures are typical of those that families put on their 'wayward' members, I will help you to generalize from Aaron's experience.

Aaron dealt with such manipulation in a number of ways.

Dealing with manipulation through guilt

When Aaron told his parents that he was going out with a non-Jewish woman their initial response was one of shock and disbelief. They then thought it was just a sexual fling, but when they had digested the reality that the relationship was serious and likely to be ongoing, they tried to manipulate Aaron to 'come back to the fold' (as one of his uncles put it) through attempting to make him feel guilty.

As I discussed in my book *Overcoming Guilt* (Sheldon Press, 1994), guilt has a number of elements. I will use RECBT's ABC framework to outline these features (see Table 6.1).

Table 6.1 Elements of guilt

ABC	Belief
'A'	I am doing the wrong thing I am failing to do the right thing I am hurting the feelings of another person (other people)
'B'	I must not do the wrong thing and I am bad if I do I must do the right thing and I am bad if I don't I must not hurt others' feelings and I am bad if I do
'C' (emotional) (behavioural)	Guilt Begging the other for forgiveness Changing my behaviour so that I am deemed acceptable

Aaron's family tried to make him feel guilty by telling him that:

- he was doing the wrong thing by going out with a non-Jewish woman because he was going against the dictates of Judaism;
- his actions were 'destroying' his family and causing them great distress.

From the perspective of RECBT, Aaron's family were providing him with invitations to accept these 'A's as reality, trusting that if he did accept them he would bring a set of irrational beliefs and would feel guilty as a result. They also assumed that if Aaron did feel guilty he would attempt to get rid of his guilty feelings by ending the relationship with Samantha and by 'returning to the fold'.

Recognizing that life is complex, not simple

When you experience guilt you tend to see the world in black and white: this is right, that is wrong. This is how Aaron's family saw the world with respect to this issue. From their perspective, Aaron's decision to go out with a non-Jewish woman was wrong, no two ways about it. The only way, therefore, that he could do the right thing was to end the relationship and only date Jewish women in future. This was the view of the world that Aaron's family were trying to get him to accept. They stressed the importance of upholding Jewish values. They reminded him of the sacrifices his fellow Jews made in the Holocaust. Indeed, one uncle told Aaron: 'You owe it to the memories of those who died in the concentration camp to end your relationship with this woman.'

Fortunately, Aaron did not see matters from this black-and-white view of the world. He did recognize that it was wrong from the perspective of Jewish law and tradition for him to marry out of the religion. However, he also thought that it was wrong to deny oneself loving and marrying one's soul mate even if she was non-Jewish. He could see that by doing the right thing he could also not escape from doing the wrong thing. Thus, if he gave up Samantha, he was doing the right thing from a Jewish perspective but the wrong thing from the perspective of his happiness. Similarly, if he married Samantha, he was doing the right thing from a happiness perspective and the wrong thing from the Jewish perspective. This relative view of matters helped him to develop a rational belief about doing wrong.

He also brought the same analysis to the issue of hurting his family. He recognized that, given their views, his immediate and extended family members were bound to feel hurt and upset with him for developing a relationship with a non-Jewish woman. However, he also knew that he would be hurt and upset if he gave her up. He further recognized that if he did give up Samantha he would be hurting her feelings as well. He accepted, therefore, that he was in a situation in which nobody could escape feeling hurt and upset.

Developing a set of rational beliefs about wrongdoing and hurting others' feelings

In this book, I have argued that the core of developing inner strength is the development of a set of rational beliefs in the face of adversity that are flexible and non-extreme in nature. In this case, Aaron developed the following rational beliefs about wrongdoing and hurting the feelings of others.

1 'I really don't want to do the wrong thing, but I am not immune from doing so and nor do I have to be. I am a fallible human being when I do the wrong thing, and not a bad person.' Holding this belief helped Aaron to sustain the view, discussed above, that he was in a situation where he could not avoid doing the wrong thing.

2 'I really don't want to hurt people's feelings, but I am not immune from doing so and nor do I have to be. I am a fallible human being when I do hurt people's feelings, and not a bad person.' Holding this belief helped Aaron to sustain the view, discussed above, that he was in a situation where he could not avoid hurting the feelings of people involved.

Developing a flexible approach to healthy self-interest and selfishness

When Aaron's family's attempts to influence him to 'return to the fold' through guilt-based manipulations failed, they began to tell him that he was selfish for putting himself first over his family and his Jewish heritage. Fortunately, Aaron resisted accepting the message made explicit in these communications (i.e. 'You are selfish for putting yourself first. Prove you are not selfish by giving up your non-Jewish girlfriend'). He did this by developing a healthy and flexible approach to the issue of healthy self-interest and selfishness. This approach is summed up below.

Selfishness, selflessness and healthy self-interest

There are three positions to be borne in mind when considering whether you are being selfish or acting in your own healthy self-interests.

- *Selfishness* Cynically putting yourself first without really thinking of others and the impact that your decisions will have on these other people.
- *Selflessness* Putting the interests of others ahead of your own interests.
- *Healthy self-interest* Recognizing that if you do not look after your important interests then others are unlikely to. This position does not preclude you from putting other people's interests before your own if their need is greater than yours.

By this definition, Aaron was acting in his own healthy interests by deciding to develop a relationship with Samantha, in that his happiness and that of Samantha was at stake. Aaron argued that if he did not take action in the service of his own happiness, then his family were unlikely to do so.

In taking this stance, Aaron did not rule out putting his family's interests above his own on other matters, but just not on this issue which he considered so vital to his own happiness.

Learning from Aaron's experience

If you are at significant odds with your family and they are trying to manipulate you through guilt, you can learn the following lessons from Aaron's experience.

1 Recognize that your family's view that you are definitely wrong is over-simplistic. You may be wrong from their

perspective but right from your own. You don't have to see the world through their eyes. Rather, you can see that the world is far more complex than the 'We are right, you are wrong' position taken by your family.

2 You are not immune from wrongdoing or hurting others' feelings and nor do you have to have such immunity. If you are doing the wrong thing from your family's perspective and if they feel hurt as a result, this is sad, but it does not mean that you are a bad person for your contribution to this. You are a fallible human being struggling to find happiness in this world, and while it would be nice to have your family's support in this, you don't have to have it.

3 When your happiness is at stake, putting yourself first is not being selfish, even if your family accuse you of this. Rather, you are acting in your own healthy interests. This does not preclude you from putting your family first on other issues.

Dealing with disapproval

When it became clear that Aaron's family could not manipulate him through guilt, they told his friends and his wider community that he had developed a serious relationship with a non-Jewish woman. As a result, Aaron began to notice that an increasing number of people he knew showed, in different ways, that they disapproved of him. Some refused to talk to him, some were openly hostile to him and yet others began to campaign to withdraw his synagogue membership.

Aaron was prepared for this and had developed the following set of rational beliefs about disapproval to help him to have the inner strength to withstand these responses:

> I would very much prefer it if people that I know and care about do not show that they disapprove of me for being in love with Samantha, but sadly and regretfully that does not mean that they must not disapprove of me. Their disapproval does not mean that I am worthless. I am still the same fallible person whether they

approve of me or not. Also, while it is a struggle for me to tolerate their disapproval, I can do so and it is worth it to me to do so.

Holding this set of rational beliefs, Aaron felt sad but not depressed about the disapproval he received from his family, friends and members of the synagogue community. These beliefs also helped him to react in a constructive manner to instances when people showed that they disapproved of him. Rather than go on the defensive or try to explain his position, all Aaron said in response was something like: 'I appreciate that you are very upset with me and I wish you could understand my position, but sadly you don't have to do so.' Note that this statement is, in fact, a verbalization of a rational flexible belief. Once he had made such a statement, Aaron then refused to get drawn into any explanation of his behaviour, even though this generally irritated the other person.

Learning from Aaron's experience

Drawing on Aaron's experience, it is important that you do the following:

1 Develop a set of rational beliefs about receiving disapproval from family members and others when you continue to act in ways that they find offensive and cannot accept. These beliefs involve you preferring that they do not disapprove of you but not demanding that they must not, judging such disapproval as bad but not the end of the world, tolerating the disapproval as you continue to plough your own furrow, and refusing to define yourself by such disapproval.

2 Act in ways that will strengthen your conviction in this belief. This may involve you articulating your rational belief where you indicate your preference to the other person, but tell him (in this case) that he does not have to meet your preference.

3 It is best not to respond to your family members' requests for you to explain your position unless they show genuine signs

of wishing to understand things from your perspective. If they do not, they will just use your engagement with them as a further attempt to get you to do what they want you to do.

Dealing with the threat of ostracism

If manipulation through guilt and various forms of disapproval have not worked to bring you back to the fold, then your family may 'up the ante' and threaten to ostracize you. This is what happened with Aaron. He received a letter from his parents which said that if he did not give up his relationship with Samantha then nobody in his family would have any contact with him again and his father would say kaddish (the prayer for the dead) for him. In the Jewish religion this effectively means that his father would be saying that Aaron was dead to him.

Aaron was thus faced with a stark decision: choose the woman he loved or choose his family, whom he also loved. Aaron chose Samantha. He wrote to his parents outlining his decision, saying that he had chosen to live his life his own way and not his parents' way. Here is how Aaron dealt with the threat of ostracism. As before, he developed the following rational belief:

> I really don't want to lose my family, but I am not immune from such a loss and nor do I have to be. I am determined to live my life my own way and I will do so even if it means being ostracized by my family. My family are very important, but they are not all-important. When it comes to a stark choice between living my own life and losing my family or keeping my family and giving up my chance of happiness, I will very, very reluctantly decide to take the course of action that will mean being ostracized by my family.

Aaron made his decision and did indeed lose his family. He married Samantha and they had two children. Aaron advanced in his career and built up a new circle of friends. While he was happy with Samantha, he had an enduring sense of sadness about the loss of a family. Choosing to live one's life one's own way generally comes at a cost but, as Aaron would say, it is worth it.

Learning from Aaron's experience

You can learn the following from Aaron's experience:

1 Once again it is important that you develop a set of rational beliefs about being ostracized by your family. Thus, you need to acknowledge that such ostracism would be highly undesirable, but that does not mean that it must not happen. It would be tragic, to be sure, but not the end of the world, and you can withstand it because you have a life to lead and you have chosen to live it in order to follow principles that you hold very dear.

2 Finally, being ostracized by your family indicates that your relationship, from their perspective, has irretrievably broken down, but that does not make you worthless. You can accept yourself in the face of such ostracism even though it is very difficult to do so.

Please note that although in this chapter I have described a situation in which Aaron chose to be ostracized by his family in order to be with the woman he loved, there are other situations in which a person chooses family above his or her principles, where he or she feels that these principles are less important than family. The point I want to stress here is that it is important to be flexible about your principles so that you can make an informed and rational decision concerning what to do when your family threaten to ostracize you if you pursue your own way.

Summary

In this chapter, I have discussed how you can deal effectively with family pressure when what you want to do conflicts with what they want you to do. I have shown you how to deal with manipulation through guilt, escalating disapproval and the threat of ostracism. It is important that you develop and maintain a set of rational beliefs about such adversities so that you can make clear rational decisions at every stage. Inner strength will help you deal with resisting invitations to feel guilty, and aid you in keeping a clear head about how to respond to disapproval so that you don't get caught up in pointless arguments. Finally, if the worst comes to the worst, inner strength will help you to get on with your life, albeit with pain and sadness, when you have been ostracized by your family for choosing to live a life that they are unable to sanction.

In the next chapter, I will discuss the inner strength you will need to develop and maintain healthy boundaries in your life.

7

How to assert healthy boundaries

Introduction

If you have ever bought a house, you will know how important boundaries are, for they make clear what belongs to you and what belongs to your neighbours. Many court cases and neighbourhood feuds have been fought over different interpretations of where boundary lines are, and people argue interpersonally and legally over who owns what.

From a psychological perspective boundaries are equally if not more important, for if you are clear but yet flexible about your psychological boundaries and if you have the inner strength to protect your boundaries when they are under attack, then it is likely that you will be psychologically healthy. In this chapter, I will discuss both interpersonal boundaries (i.e. boundaries between you and other people) and intrapersonal boundaries (i.e. boundaries between different parts of you). Then I will discuss the major problems that people have with respect to their psychological boundaries of both types and will show that these can be effectively addressed. Briefly, these problems are:

- not knowing where your boundaries should lie;
- having an unrealistic idea of where your boundaries should lie;
- knowing where your boundaries should lie, but not asserting them;
- knowing where your boundaries should lie, but being rigid about asserting them.

What are healthy boundaries?

It is not my intention in this book to tell you how to live your life. Perish the thought! However, in my experience of working with people in a variety of settings, it is my view that healthy boundaries have a number of defining features.

Healthy boundaries provide a balance between the pursuit of short-term goals and long-term goals

In Chapter 3, I argued that we have three 'selves'; a short-term self which is concerned with our pursuit of immediate pleasure and comfort and the relief of immediate pain and discomfort; a long-term self which is concerned with the pursuit of our long-term goals; and an executive self that is concerned with mediating between these other two selves when they are in conflict.

When we have healthy boundaries in the area of our goals, we know when we should be pursuing our long-term goals and when we are defeating ourselves by pursuing our short-term goals instead. They also specify when it is acceptable for us to pursue our short-term goals. Our healthy boundaries, therefore, show us how we can pursue both our short-term and long-term goals in a balanced way.

Healthy boundaries facilitate the good use of time

In modern life, we generally have many tasks to do and a limited time in which to do them. Having healthy boundaries with respect to time means that we tend to use time efficiently in that we know what we need to do and when we need to do it. In this context, the term 'time management' makes little sense, for time does not need to be managed. A better term is 'self-management within the context of time' since it places the onus on us in managing how we use our time.

Healthy boundaries reflect the philosophy of healthy self-interest

In Chapter 6, I introduced the concept of healthy self-interest. I see this as a philosophy whereby you look after your own healthy interests when it is important for you to do so, and in implementing this you do your best to minimize the pain and inconvenience that others may experience as a result. You also are prepared to help others pursue their healthy interests whenever you can. As you can see, healthy self-interest is a flexible position. Healthy boundaries enable you to know when to pursue your interests and when to help people achieve theirs.

Healthy boundaries facilitate role-appropriate behaviour

In life, we occupy a number of roles (e.g. parent, son or daughter, in-law, lecturer and student). While it is possible to discharge these roles in different ways, having healthy boundaries with respect to roles means that we tend to act in ways that would be generally regarded as appropriate to the role we are occupying rather than in ways more in keeping with the complementary role. Thus, if you are a mother of a 12-year-old child, keeping a healthy boundary with respect to roles would mean that you would be acting in ways consistent with your parenting role. When a 12-year-old adopts a parenting role towards his or her own mother because the latter has a drug problem, this would be seen as a healthy boundary being violated by the mother's failure to look after herself. Problems are very likely to occur when this happens.

Healthy boundaries prevent abuse in relationships

If you have healthy boundaries with respect to your relationships this generally prevents abuse in all its forms from happening in these relationships. Thus, when a parent sexually abuses a child or a lecturer has sex with a student, these violations are generally the result of the person with the power in the relationship overstepping what would be regarded as a healthy boundary in the relationship. In general, the person with the power in a relationship acts in a way that violates the healthy boundary and the person with less power is the victim of the boundary violation.

Dealing with problems with respect to healthy boundaries

People experience a variety of problems that prevent them from having the inner strength to keep to healthy boundaries, and in this section of the chapter I will discuss these problems and show you how you can address them if they apply to you.

Not knowing where your healthy boundaries should lie

It may be that you don't know where your healthy boundaries should lie. If this is the case, it may be because you have not had any good models for such boundaries or because your emotional problems have blocked you from learning where such boundaries should exist. While it may be useful for you to understand the reason or reasons why you have not developed a clear idea of where your healthy boundaries should lie, such understanding may not, in itself, help you to identify where they actually should lie. So how can you identify where they should lie in your case? I suggest that you first make a list of areas in your life which require the development of healthy boundaries. These may include the following:

- *Your use of time to engage in a variety of tasks and activities* You will generally assign more time to tasks that have greater priority for you.
- *Your pursuit of goals, both short-term and long-term* As mentioned above, healthy boundaries in this area allow you to meet both in a balanced way.

- *The roles that you occupy* Using the philosophy of healthy self-interest, write down your behaviour that reflects keeping to healthy boundaries while occupying these roles and your behaviour that fails to keep to them or violates them.
- *The relationships you have with people where these differ from the above* Again, using the philosophy of healthy self-interest, write down your behaviour that reflects keeping to healthy boundaries in these relationships and your behaviour that fails to keep to them or violates them.

If you have problems doing this I suggest that you do the following:

1 Ask people you know and trust for advice concerning where you should draw your healthy boundaries. Collate this information and develop a list of boundaries which best suits you.
2 Think of someone in your life that you trust, who knows you well, cares for you and has your best interests at heart. What advice would this person give you concerning where to draw your healthy boundaries? Write this advice down and modify the points to better fit your own situation.
3 Think of someone you know well, care for and whose best interests you have at heart. What advice would you give this person concerning where to draw his or her healthy boundaries? Write this advice down and then apply it to yourself, modifying the points to better fit your own situation.

Having an unrealistic idea of where your healthy boundaries should lie

People tend to make two major errors when thinking of what constitutes their healthy boundaries: their boundaries reflect either a philosophy of low self-esteem or an inflated sense of self-importance.

Boundaries that reflect a philosophy of low self-esteem

If your boundaries reflect a philosophy of low self-esteem, on close inspection you will see that they are not healthy because they do not reflect what is truly important to you (i.e. your major life's goals and priorities). You think so little of yourself that you tend to have boundaries where you only allow yourself to pursue what really matters to you in life when you have helped others to achieve their goals or when you have taken care of the drudgery of life. In a phrase, your boundaries are dictated by a 'me last' view of the world.

What you need to do is to take your boundaries and rewrite them as if you accept yourself as having equal worth to others and are adopting the philosophy of healthy self-interest. When you rewrite these boundaries, make sure that you are putting yourself first in areas that are important to you before you attend to the needs of others. Remind yourself that because other people have goals that are important to them, it does not follow that you should drop the pursuit of your own goals and attend to theirs unless there is a good, objective reason to do so. Also, make sure that at times you attend to your pleasure before you take care of life's chores. In the next section, I will discuss low self-esteem as an obstacle to you asserting your healthy boundaries and show you how you can effectively address this issue.

Boundaries that reflect an inflated sense of self-importance

If your boundaries reflect an inflated sense of self-importance, on close inspection you will see that they are not healthy because they only reflect what is truly important to you. You think so highly of yourself that you tend to have boundaries where you allow yourself to pursue only what really matters to you in life and place little or no value in helping others to achieve their goals or in taking care of the drudgery of life. On this latter point, you either don't do mundane chores or expect others to do them for you. In a phrase, your boundaries are dictated by a 'me first' view of the world.

What you need to do is to take your boundaries and rewrite them as if you accept others as having equal worth to yourself and are adopting the philosophy of healthy self-interest. When you rewrite these boundaries, make sure that you are putting others first in areas that are very important to them before you attend to your less important desires. Remind yourself that because you have goals that are important to you, it does not follow that you should always pursue them. Also, make sure at times that you attend to life's chores before you take care of meeting your desires. Do not expect others to pick up after you.

Giving up an inflated sense of self-importance is difficult because it is unlikely that you will recognize this description of yourself even if it is true. It may be that you will only seek help on this issue when others refuse to go along with you regarding it. If they follow my advice in the next section, they will refuse!

Knowing where your healthy boundaries should lie, but not asserting them

In this section, I will assume that you know what your healthy boundaries are but lack the inner strength to assert them. I will illustrate my discussion by considering the case of Fiona.

Fiona was in many ways a model employee. She worked hard, was competent at what she did and was always willing to lend a helping hand to her co-workers and to her boss. The problem was that everyone tended to take advantage of her, and recently she had wanted to assert her healthy boundaries (which she had come to appreciate with the help of two of her good friends) but lacked the inner strength to do so.

In RECBT, we recommend that the best way of beginning to address your inner strength failure to assert healthy boundaries is to take a specific example of such lack of inner strength and to use the Situational ABC framework to assess the example (see Chapter 4).

Here is how Fiona assessed a typical example of her lack of inner strength to assert her healthy boundaries.

'Situation' = My boss asked me to stay behind and work for an extra two hours when I had already made plans to take my mother shopping

'A' = He will be cross if I say no
'B' = My boss must not be cross with me. If he is it proves I am worthless.
'C' (emotional) = Anxiety
(behavioural) = Agreeing to work the extra two hours

The next step is to use the same framework to outline how you would have demonstrated inner strength and asserted your healthy boundaries and, in particular, to specify the rational beliefs that would have enabled you to have done this. Here is Fiona's Situational ABC analysis of her inner strength-based goals.

'Situation' = My boss asked me to stay behind and work for an extra two hours when I had already made plans to take my mother shopping

'A' = He will be cross if I say no
'B' = I don't want my boss to be cross with me, but he doesn't have to react in the way that I want. If he is cross with me that will be unpleasant, but it does not prove that I am worthless. I am the same fallible human being whether he is cross with me or not.
'C' (emotional) = Concerned, but not anxious
(behavioural) = Say no to my boss's request rather than agree to work the extra two hours

If you compare Fiona's Situational ABC assessment of her failure to show inner strength and assert her healthy boundary with her boss with that of her inner strength-based goal, you will notice that the 'situation' and 'A' are the same but that the 'B' and the 'C' are different. This is important since it may well be true that Fiona's boss will be cross with her. She is not in control of how he responds. She is only in control of how she thinks and chooses to act in response to his behaviour, and thus the only goals that she can set concern changes at 'B' and at 'C'. This is the essence of inner strength. Consequently, when using the Situational ABC framework to assess your problem response and your inner strength-based goal, assume temporarily that your inference at 'A' is correct.

The next step is to question your rational and irrational beliefs. This is how Fiona questioned hers.

> It is true that I don't want my boss to be cross with me when I assert my healthy boundaries and say no to his request, but it is also true that he doesn't have to respond in the way that I want. It is not sensible for me to conclude that he must do what I want. He has the freedom to respond as he wants. However, if I do demand that he is not cross with me then I will not assert my healthy boundaries, whereas if I prefer but do not demand that he is not cross, I will assert myself. Also, if he is cross with me, his response cannot define my worth. I am in charge of that and I can prove that I am the same fallible, unrateable human being whether he is cross with me or not. It is illogical for me to define the whole of myself on the basis of another person's response. Also, if I allow him to define my worth then I will not assert my healthy boundaries, whereas if I accept myself, I will assert myself.

The main way that you can internalize the rational beliefs that are at the core of inner strength is to act on them. The next step, therefore, is for you to behave according to your healthy boundaries while rehearsing your rational beliefs. This is exactly what Fiona did.

> Fiona resolved to demonstrate inner strength and assert her healthy boundaries whenever she thought that her boss or her colleagues were attempting to take advantage of her good nature. At first, Fiona found doing so uncomfortable but she persisted and soon her boss and colleagues stopped trying to take advantage of her and began to respect her boundaries. This is not to say that she never agreed to work late or to help her colleagues. However, she did so not because she thought

that she had to or that doing so prevented her from thinking of herself as worthless. Rather, she did so when it was clear that these others genuinely needed her help and were not taking advantage of her.

This is a common occurrence. When you assert your boundaries firmly but flexibly, others are more likely to respect you and less likely to abuse you than before.

Note the way Fiona generalized her learning from a specific example of her failure to show inner strength and keep to her healthy boundaries to a more general, flexible assertion of these boundaries. You can follow Fiona's lead and use the 'specific to general' guideline with each of your obstacles to maintaining healthy boundaries.

I mentioned earlier that people who feel powerless in situations are particularly prone to not asserting their healthy boundaries. However, while it may be that certain roles are invested with more power than other complementary roles, it is important that you do not forget that you have personal power which only you can wield or surrender. It is a mark of inner strength when you use your personal power to assert your healthy boundaries where the other person has more role power than you. It may be that you will experience a negative outcome if you assert these boundaries, but your irrational beliefs often lead you to exaggerate the negative consequences of your assertion. However, if you do experience a negative outcome which is unjust you can also use your inner strength to stand up for yourself and to fight for what you believe in, as I discussed in Chapter 5.

Knowing where your healthy boundaries should lie, but being rigid about asserting them

One of the fascinating characteristics of human beings is our ability to take a good idea (e.g. the assertion of healthy boundaries) and make it bad by being rigid about it. Thus, you may think that it is a healthy boundary not to agree to work extra hours when your boss asks you to do so, and you may well be correct. However, if you believe that you must never agree to violate this boundary then you are taking a good idea and turning it into a dogma. Occasionally you could be helpful to your employer by working a few extra hours, to get an important order out, for example. If you are rigid about not doing so then you won't do so. However, if you are flexible about asserting your healthy boundary, then you will probably help out since you recognize that it is a one-off event.

There are different forms of rigidity about keeping to healthy boundaries. Here are the most common:

- *Rigidity based on perfectionism* Here, you regard the achievement of a healthy boundary as the perfect standard which you believe you have to achieve.
- *Obsessive–compulsive rigidity* Here, you believe that you have to assert your healthy boundary otherwise chaos will ensue.
- *Discomfort-based rigidity* Here, the assertion of your healthy boundary gives you a sense of comfort and you believe that you must not experience discomfort.

Developing inner strength with respect to asserting boundaries not only involves you overcoming the obstacles to such assertion, it also involves you overcoming your rigidity about keeping to healthy boundaries. To do this you need to construct a rational belief about healthy boundaries, such as: 'It is desirable for me to assert my healthy boundaries, but I do not always have to do so. There may be times when it is useful for me to break my boundary, and when I do this I can tolerate the discomfort (or the fact that I am not acting perfectly) even if it is a struggle for me to do so.' It is, of course, important for you to act on this rational belief in order for you to strengthen your conviction in it.

Summary

In this chapter, I have outlined the importance of you asserting healthy boundaries both intrapersonally (where you are clear when to meet your short-term goals and when to work towards your long-term goals) and interpersonally (i.e. in your relationships with other people, particularly to avoid being exploited or even abused). I showed you how to overcome your obstacles to healthy boundary assertion and show inner strength by keeping to these boundaries, particularly in the face of adversity. Finally, I cautioned you against being rigid about asserting your healthy boundaries, arguing that there will be times when it is useful for you to act against these boundaries. In the final chapter in this book, I will consider how you can deal with the lapses that you will experience as you work towards developing inner strength and how to prevent relapse in this area of human endeavour.

8

Dealing with lapses in inner strength and preventing relapse

Introduction

Having made progress in developing your inner strength, it is vital to deal with lapses to continued inner strength and to prevent any relapse. I regard a *lapse*, in this context, as a temporary non-serious return to a state where you lack inner strength. A *relapse*, on the other hand, is a more permanent and serious return to that state. To prevent such a relapse I suggest you follow the relapse prevention sequence.

The relapse prevention sequence and how to use it

Please remember that the following sequence of steps in this suggested method for ensuring prevention of relapse and the order in which I have presented them are simply a suggestion and you do not need to follow them slavishly. They should be used merely as a guide, which you can modify to suit your own circumstances.

The twelve steps

Step 1: Review your present achievement in developing inner strength

This first step in the relapse prevention sequence relates to your progress up until now in developing your inner strength. To take effective action in dealing with your relapse you first need to appreciate what you have achieved so far. You may also find it helpful to think back on what you have learned that has enabled you to progress in your development of inner strength.

Step 2: Think through how you can apply what you have learned to future situations to test your inner strength

Using the knowledge acquired from Step 1 you can now begin to think through how you may be able to apply this learning to problems you may encounter in the future.

Step 3: Develop rational beliefs about lapses

At the beginning of this chapter I defined a lapse as a temporary and non-serious return to a state where you fail to show inner strength. It is quite likely that you will experience a number of such lapses in your journey to developing inner strength. What is important is that you develop rational beliefs about experiencing such lapses. By doing so you will learn from them.

On the other hand, if you have a set of irrational beliefs about lapsing then you may disturb yourself about doing so, and this will prevent you from learning from these lapses, thus increasing the chances of experiencing a relapse, which I define as a more enduring, serious return to a state where you fail to demonstrate inner strength.

The following is a set of rational beliefs which you can adapt for your own use in thinking about and responding to the lapses that will inevitably occur on your journey to developing inner strength.

- I would rather not experience lapses in inner strength but I am not immune from them, nor do I have to be.
- It is unfortunate to experience lapses in inner strength, but it isn't the end of the world.
- It is a struggle to tolerate lapses in my inner strength, but I can put up with them and doing so is worth it.
- I am a fallible human being. I will experience lapses along the

way to developing inner strength and doing so doesn't make
me less of a person.

- Lapses in inner strength don't make the world a rotten place.
  The world is a complex mixture of the good, the bad and the
  neutral.

If you develop this kind of rational philosophy, you will be in
the best position to deal with the main reason people relapse –
failure to deal with the factors that make them especially liable
to lapse in showing inner strength.

Step 4: Identify factors to which you remain vulnerable

Vulnerability factors are factors which, if you encounter them,
cause you to be vulnerable to responding without inner strength.
Such a vulnerability factor may be external or internal to you.
A typical external vulnerability factor would be a negative situation involving other people which you may find particularly
difficult to deal with and which tests your inner strength. So if
you want to defend something you believe in, being with other
people who strongly hold a different view and are likely to criti-
cize you for your beliefs may represent an external vulnerability
factor for you.

Internal vulnerability factors would include the urge to act in
an undisciplined way and a sense of discomfort. For instance,
supposing you were trying to cut down your alcohol intake
and you experienced the urge to drink, then this represents an
internal vulnerability factor.

The most reliable method for identifying a vulnerability
factor is to think back over times when, having made
progress, you lapsed into responses which do not show any
inner strength. If such lapses occurred in situations that
resembled each other, then a vulnerability factor is likely to
be present.

Pete, for instance, has been doing very well in dealing with a
tendency to put things off. However, in the course of a week he

procrastinated twice when his friends invited him to go out to the pub with them.

In this context, the Situational ABC framework discussed earlier in this book (see Chapter 4) should be referred to, in order to highlight the vulnerability factor. Table 8.1 shows how this framework may be applied generally in identifying a vulnerability factor, while Table 8.2 shows how Pete used it in his particular case. His vulnerability factor was rather different from the 'A's to which he originally responded with procrastination. His original 'A's involved his feeling uncomfortable when he had to get down to studying, while his vulnerability factor was the thought of having fun instead of studying.

Table 8.1 The application of the Situational ABC framework to the identification of a vulnerability factor

'Situation'	The situation in which the lapse occurred
'A'	Vulnerability factor (the aspect of the situation to which you had the unhealthy response)
'B'	Irrational beliefs
'C'	Unhealthy response

Table 8.2 How Pete applied the Situational ABC framework to the identification of his vulnerability factor

'Situation' = My friends knocked at my door and invited me to a party when I had just sat down to study, having tolerated the discomfort of doing so

'A' = Vulnerability factor = The prospect of having fun

'B' = I must not pass up the opportunity of having fun. I could not stand the deprivation if I did

'C' = Procrastination

Step 5: Determine how you would deal constructively with these vulnerability factors should you encounter them

Having used the Situational ABC framework to identify your vulnerability factor at 'A', you can carry on using it to identify and respond to the irrational beliefs at 'B', dealing with specific examples where you did not take action in regard to your vulnerability factors in ways that would indicate inner strength. You can do this in the way shown in the following step.

Step 6: Use the Situational ABC framework

- Specify your responses at 'C' which do not indicate inner strength. Such responses would include (a) an unhealthy negative emotion; (b) an unconstructive behaviour or action tendency; and, if relevant, (c) a highly distorted thought or thoughts, with a negative bias.

- Remind yourself of your vulnerability factor at 'A'.

- Identify the irrational beliefs at 'B' that underlie the above responses at 'C'. State the rigid belief and the one extreme belief that best explains your unconstructive responses. You should select either an awfulizing belief, a discomfort intolerance belief or a depreciation belief (self-, other- or life-).

- State the responses at 'C' that demonstrate inner strength and that you are aiming for when meeting your vulnerability factor at 'A'. Assuming that the vulnerability factor is a negative event, your emotional goal will be negative but healthy, your behavioural goal will be constructive and your thinking goal will be realistic.

- Identify those rational beliefs at 'B' that underlie your emotional, behavioural and thinking goals. Specify the flexible belief and the one non-extreme belief that explains most accurately the responses that indicate inner strength. You should choose either a non-awfulizing belief, a discomfort tolerance belief or an acceptance belief (self-, other- or life-).

- Examine your rational and irrational beliefs by questioning them until it is clear to you that the former are true, logical and helpful and the latter are false, illogical and unhelpful.
- Make a commitment to yourself to strengthen your rational beliefs.

Step 7: Use imagery rehearsal of rational beliefs

Having committed yourself to reinforcing the rational beliefs that underlie your desired responses (i.e. those indicating inner strength) to your vulnerability factor, you must make these rational beliefs even stronger, especially by the use of rational-emotive imagery (REI), in the following way.

- Close your eyes, imagine yourself facing your vulnerability factor and feel yourself becoming emotionally disturbed while you do so, or experience an urge to act in ways that lack inner strength.
- While you still face the vulnerability factor, change your emotional response to the way you would like to feel in relation to the factor (i.e. a healthy negative emotion) or change your urge to act into one that is driven by inner strength, and maintain that response for a few minutes.
- Make sure that you have changed your emotional response or urge to act by exchanging your irrational beliefs for their rational belief equivalents. If you have not done so, repeat the technique until you have.
- Repeat this exercise three times a day until your emotional and behavioural responses to the vulnerability factor indicate inner strength.

This is how Pete used REI to strengthen his rational beliefs:

- He closed his eyes and saw himself facing the prospect of having a great night out when his friends invited him to the pub. He made himself experience the urge to stop studying and to go with them.

- While still facing this vulnerability factor, he changed his urge to a response where he said no to his friends and returned to his studies. He allowed himself to feel very uncomfortable about the deprivation he experienced and he maintained that response for a few minutes.
- Pete then made sure that he changed his emotional response and action tendency by changing his irrational beliefs (i.e. 'I must not miss any opportunity for having a great night out. I just could not stand the deprivation if I did') to his rational belief equivalents (i.e. 'I don't want to pass up the opportunity to have a great night out, but that doesn't mean that I must not do so. I can tolerate the deprivation of doing so and it's worth it to me to do so since I want to pass my exams').
- Pete repeated this exercise three times a day until his emotional and behavioural responses to the vulnerability factor became more characterized by inner strength; in particular, instead of going to the pub, he concentrated on his studies even though this made him feel very uncomfortable.

Step 8: Use imagery rehearsal of constructive behaviour

You can also use rational-emotive imagery to rehearse seeing yourself act in ways that demonstrate inner strength when facing your vulnerability factor. Some people find this a very useful step to take before taking action in relation to their actual vulnerability factor, while for others this step is not necessary and might even be counterproductive. You may wish to try out this technique to determine for yourself whether or not it is likely to be helpful to you as a preparation for taking inner strength-based action in the real world.

If you decide to use imagery rehearsal to imagine yourself acting in a way consistent with inner strength in facing your vulnerability factor, then the more vividly you can imagine doing so, the better. You should bear in mind, however, that some people do not experience vivid imagery and if this applies to you, don't worry, since you can still use this imagery technique to your benefit in the following way:

- Select a vulnerability factor that is challenging for you to deal with, but which you don't find overwhelming.
- Be clear in your mind what your vulnerability factor is. It will probably be the 'A' in the Situational ABC framework.
- Be clear in your mind how you are going to deal constructively with this vulnerability factor.
- Choose a situation in which it is likely that you will encounter your vulnerability factor.
- Get yourself into the right frame of mind by rehearsing your relevant rational beliefs.
- Imagine yourself facing your vulnerability factor and dealing with it constructively. It is better to see yourself struggling than to see yourself showing unrealistic mastery.
- Repeat this imagery exercise three times a day until you are ready to face the vulnerability in real life.

This is how Pete used this technique:

- He imagined a scenario in which his friends would ask him out to the pub once he had just sat down to study.
- In doing this he focused on the anticipated sense of fun if he went and his sense of deprivation if he didn't go. This was challenging for him to deal with but not overwhelming, and was the 'A' in his Situational ABC framework (see Table 8.2).
- He was clear in his mind that he was not going to accept his friends' invitation even though turning it down made him feel deprived.
- He got himself into the right frame of mind by rehearsing his relevant rational beliefs, i.e. 'I don't want to pass up the opportunity to have a great night out, but that doesn't mean that I must not do so. I can tolerate the deprivation of doing so and it is worth it to me to do so since I want to pass my degree.'

- He pictured himself turning down his friends' invitation, even though he felt very uncomfortable about doing so when he imagined his loss of anticipated fun. He saw himself wavering as they put him under pressure, but in the end he saw himself declining once and for all.
- He repeated this imagery exercise three times a day until he was ready to face the vulnerability factor in reality.

Step 9: Put this constructive plan into action by facing your vulnerability factors

Now you have your rational beliefs and a clear idea of how you're going to act, you are ready to face your vulnerability factor. You can use the principle that I have called 'challenging but not overwhelming', according to which you decide that facing your vulnerability factor in a given context constitutes a challenge for you but is not overwhelming. You are not, so to speak, biting off more than you can chew by taking this step.

It is useful to get yourself in the right frame of mind by rehearsing your rational belief before you take action and to hold this belief in mind while taking action. Although the former is nearly always possible, the latter is more difficult, given that you may have to concentrate fully on what you are doing and may not have time to rehearse your rational belief when faced with the reality of the situation, even briefly. Don't worry if this is the case, since your pre-action rehearsal of your rational belief will often be enough to sustain you; if it isn't, you can review and learn from this experience later.

This is how Pete used this principle in action. He was in the common room when he heard some of his friends talking about going to the pub that night and asking him if he wanted to come. Before, he would have declined, because he knew he wanted to study and didn't want to expose himself to temptation, but as he was starting to work on his vulnerability factors he replied that he might want to go and that just before leaving for the pub themselves they should knock on his door to check with him. Pete could easily turn down an invitation to go to the pub when it was far enough in advance and he wasn't studying, but found it much more difficult to refuse such an invitation when going to the pub was imminent and it could serve as a welcome distraction from studying. In other words, the former scenario was not a vulnerability factor for him, but the latter was.

Pete then went to his room, rehearsed his rational belief and settled down to his studies. On hearing a knock at the door, he quickly reviewed his rational belief again and answered the door, but then told his friends that he had decided not to go to the pub. Following some light-hearted banter about Pete being 'boring' they went off to the pub without him. Pete felt deprived and frustrated, but told himself that he could tolerate these uncomfortable feelings and that they would pass once he had become involved in his studies, which is precisely what happened.

Step 10: Review your experiences of dealing with these vulnerability factors and learn from these reviews

Once you have taken action in the face of your vulnerability factors several times, you should stand back and review your experiences of doing so in order to learn from them. You will thus be able to fine-tune your responses to your vulnerability factors. Pete did this and realized that what was particularly helpful to him in responding to invitations to go to the pub when he should have been studying was actually admitting to his friends that he wanted to go to the pub, but that he didn't have to follow this because his plan was to study and thus he hoped they understood that he was not going to go with them. Reminding himself of this rational belief helped him to ask his friends to keep inviting him to the pub so that he could get practice at declining and thereby strengthening his conviction in his rational belief; he also even occasionally accepted their invitations, so that he wasn't strengthening his conviction in his rational belief in too rigid a manner and could still retain the right to have a night out if he so chose.

Step 11: Develop rational beliefs about relapse

As mentioned at the start of this chapter, a relapse is a more enduring, serious return to a state characterized by lack of inner strength – to put it in plain terms, going back to square one. The steps so far discussed have been those you need to take to deal with lapses and your vulnerability factors, which will thus help prevent a relapse. However, as you may relapse when it comes to exercising inner strength, it is important for you to address this possibility. Having done so, ask yourself what particular aspect of relapsing in terms of your inner strength you would disturb yourself about. This represents your 'A' in the Situational ABC framework. In my experience people disturb themselves about two major 'A's:

1 weakness (if I relapse in terms of my inner strength, it will reveal that I have a weakness);
2 loss of self-control (if I relapse in terms of my inner strength, it shows that I have lost self-control).

Develop rational beliefs about weakness-related relapse   When you disturb yourself about relapsing because you assume it reveals a weakness in you, you may experience shame which will motivate you to avoid dealing with the possibility of relapse. You may also think that people will look down on you and dismiss you should you relapse.

If you find yourself experiencing shame about relapsing it's important to adopt the following rational beliefs, which you should express in your own words.

- *Flexible belief*: 'I really don't want to be weak and relapse, but sadly and regretfully I am not immune from doing so; nor is there any need for me to be so immune.'
- *Non-awfulizing belief*: 'If I were to be weak and relapse, while it would be unfortunate, it would not be the end of the world.'
- *Discomfort tolerance belief*: 'I may find it difficult to put up with being weak and relapsing, but I am prepared to tolerate it and it will be worth it to me to do so.'
- *Self-acceptance belief*: 'It would be bad if I were to relapse, but it wouldn't prove that I'm a weak or pathetic person. It simply means that I am a complex, fallible human being.'

Develop rational beliefs about relapse related to loss of self-control If you disturb yourself about relapsing because it suggests that you have experienced a loss of self-control, you may tend to experience anxiety which could lead you to make a desperate attempt to regain such self-control. However, given that your attempt is based on desperation it may lead you to become more anxious rather than less anxious, thus increasing the negativity of your subsequent thoughts about the extent and implications of such a loss of self-control (i.e. your subsequent thinking will become highly distorted and skewed to the negative).

If you experience anxiety about the loss of self-control that accompanies relapse, then it's again important that you develop the following rational beliefs which, again, you should express in your own words.

- *Flexible belief*: 'I really don't want to relapse and lose self-control, but sadly and regretfully I am not immune from doing so, nor is there any need for me to be immune.'
- *Non-awfulizing belief*: 'If I were to relapse and lose-self-control, while it would be unfortunate, it would not be the end of the world.'

- *Discomfort tolerance belief*: 'I may find it difficult to put up with relapsing and losing self-control, but I am prepared to tolerate it and it will be worth it to me to do so.'
- *Life-acceptance belief*: 'It would be bad if I were to relapse and lose self-control, but it wouldn't prove that life is all bad for allowing this to happen to me. Life is a complex mixture of the good, the bad and the neutral.'

Develop rational beliefs about relapse in general I have now dealt with two of the most common problems that people tend to have about relapsing with respect to inner strength (i.e. being weak and losing self-control) and I have outlined the rational beliefs you need to develop if you experience one or both of these issues. However, some people disturb themselves about the act of relapsing itself, and if this applies to you it will be important for you to develop a set of rational beliefs about the fact of relapse itself in the area of inner strength. I will list these here, but suggest that you modify them to suit your own situation.

- *Flexible belief*: 'I really don't want to relapse, but sadly and regretfully I am not immune from it, nor is there any need for me to be immune.'
- *Non-awfulizing belief*: 'If I were to relapse, while it would be unfortunate, it would not be the end of the world.'
- *Discomfort tolerance belief*: 'I may find it difficult to put up with relapsing, but I am prepared to tolerate it and it will be worth it to me to do so.'
- *Self-acceptance belief*: 'It would be bad if I were to relapse, but it wouldn't prove that I am a weak, pathetic person. It means that I am a complex, fallible human being.'
- *Life-acceptance belief*: 'Life isn't bad if I relapse. It is a complex place where many good, bad and neutral things happen, including relapse.'

Step 12: Learn from relapse

If you develop and implement a rational philosophy about the relapse of your inner strength, then you will calm down about the prospect of its happening. This will help you put the likelihood of your relapsing into perspective, and will also help you realize that you will lessen the chance of doing so if you are diligent in learning from your relapses and deal sufficiently with your vulnerability factors.

Your rational philosophy will also help you learn from the experience of a relapse in inner strength should this happen to you. It will help you to review times where your inner strength lapses became more serious, and what you should have done to deal with these effectively, thus reducing the chances of relapse. Then you would implement this learning, thus helping you to protect yourself from relapsing in future.

Summary

In any process of personal change, it is important to accept that lapses are an inevitable part of this development. I consider developing rational beliefs about lapses as the best way to deal with them. Moreover, to prevent relapse you must deal with and learn from your lapses. Most importantly, relapse prevention depends on your identifying and dealing effectively with your vulnerability factors. You can prepare yourself to face your vulnerability factors by using the Situational ABC framework and by employing imagery. When you face your vulnerability factors in real life, you can use the 'challenging but not overwhelming' concept and rehearse relevant rational beliefs before and during the experience. As is the case with lapses, it is best to develop rational beliefs about relapse. If you do, you are less likely to relapse than if you had held irrational beliefs about it. However, if you do relapse, rather than disturbing yourself about this grim reality, learn from it.

We have now reached the end of the book. I hope you have found it helpful and if you have any feedback, please write to me care of Sheldon Press.

Index